1

To Barb.
I hope you
enjoy it.
Gary Kendall

ASPARAGUS IN MY TUBA

The Strains of an Absentee Gardener

A Book of Personal Essays and Remembrances

by

Gary Kendall

Table of Contents

Introduction

Nature And True Nature

When the Call came, I slammed the mouthpiece down and rushed out; it was the kind of thing I loved and I wasn't about to miss it. A second one followed. It found me off fishing somewhere, and I didn't return the Call. Ah, but switchboard operators didn't throw in the towel easily. Again it shattered the silence, tolling for what I knew would be my last chance. Somehow I managed the good sense to at least put it on hold. But then.... a good quarter of a century is a long time for *Call-Waiting.*

The Call was—what else?—that of The Wild, of things synonymous to life, of God's purest beauty, of nature and country, of that great leveler, the soft, loamy earth, into which you simply itch to plunge your hands; and of my first actual job, farming. This was the stuff: pithy, circumstantial evidence of my True Nature, if not always so easily flushed into the permanent light of day. The geezer I worked for was a parishioner of my grandfather's *Church in the Wildwood,* also the most backward farmer in that part of Missouri. Other, more progressive "Aggies"* noticed my affinity for country ways but were scared off by the in-town upbringing. Considerate of them to not get me maimed, their caution nevertheless knocked my phone on off the hook, well nigh disconnecting the service.

By the grand old age of twenty, my True Nature and I had drifted apart. Heartthrobs and fantasies intervened. Mine was a host of talents, if not the moxie to carry through. Perhaps the most salient of these, music, eventually led me to classical singing. What I accomplished, while not at all bad, didn't exactly ignite the world. After a decade of fighting through it, I took a tenure-track position at one of the better American music schools, joining, as it were, the fraternity of mid-career "give backers."

And yet... the globe only smoldered. Having stood in the shadow of a college long enough to be born and raised there, it was surprising how the other side of a desk struck me. That cup of tea went

**Derogatory University of Missouri nickname for agriculture majors.

from lukewarm to bitter in quick order, my "banana peel" promotions
and lifelong didactic penchant notwithstanding. To the *shock and awe*
of almost everyone in my circle, I walked away, electing a riskier path:
big city private voice teaching, though with the now indispensable trips
to the outer banks of Beulah Land.

But my guardian angel's mission would be fulfilled. From the
onset, no argument for putting myself in *teaching's way* was more
compelling than disinterring a long-awaited place in the sun. The sylvan
jumper cables were well oiled; extended stay on the Swedish
countryside had long since seen to that.

In my third faculty year, I bought a run-down historic home and
some acreage toward the northeastern corner of Kentucky. Coppertone
spout up, I prepared to rub—and drink—it all in: my True Nature had
reclaimed me heart and soul.

But the path to the cow path would not be smooth. The esthete
agrarian days of Jefferson, all the way to Serkin* and Solzhenitsyn,

*The great Czech concert pianist, who preferred to live on his farm in Vermont.
He was once presented with a new Farmall tractor by the Philadelphia Orchestra. Solzhenitsyn,
in exile from Russia, also lived on a farm in Vermont.

.

were in the history books. Yokels did that kind of thing, one man's paradise empowering another's gibes: "Gary Kendall, PHM—Purveyor of Horse Manure" (extended family members); "Let's get out of this jungle" (former in-laws); "Arlene** *loves* it out there! What do you *do* all day?" (current in-laws); "What kind of person would *live* out here?" (students). That which we were all born to, in a high-ticket, pseudo-sophisticate world was suddenly anathema.

Since such time, I have sought adjunct ways to survive in the real wild, the tame wild, the shouldn't-be-wild, as opposed to the gradual deforestation of the classical music scene. Such is reality, *my* reality, and I learned the hard way you can but thwart it so long before

In my greater serenity I was also poorer, my joints stiffer, my energies diminished. And yet, the dust-covered Call button faintly glowed, the grist for my long-enjoyed essays and other tales heaped deeper, if now slanted toward the simpler bucolic existence, and a singer's memoirs.

There is no one qute like me on the still partially green contours; or like *us*.

** My wife

Arlene and I often mused on just how many people in that borderline Confederate commonwealth were similarly engaged almost any evening: discoursing on art or history, sampling an international dish *al fresco* to the tune of a Schumann Symphony, all the while projecting a time frame for the cows' coming "fresh." That is, until driven by commitment or God's owfan air conditioning, we shove off along the camel route to New York.

Nor is the Darling offended by my desire for hermitage, decoded by near melanoma-inducing chores on the DB-880 tractor, or my going up in smoke with a premium *maduro** at the "Laughing Place."** She knows those two things approach a similar category as loving her, that they teach me more about me than just about anything else, and that I promise, in one sound piece, to return anon.

The first time I saw morning river fog rolling up the valley behind our Arcadian home, I ran screaming for any housebound creature willing to behold the marvel. "You'll never see it again," I

*A dark, strong cigar
**A special location in the woods where I occasionally go. "The Laughing Place," is borrowed from the "Uncle Remus" children's stories

yelled. For once the sleepers were right to ignore me. Like pea soup, the mysterious murk billows up a couple of times a month, looking like my idea of *Valhalla.*

At least I think so. Instead of standing there like the *Incredible Shrinking Man,* infusing its moisture into my once singerly capillaries, I'm often still "out fishing". But casting about the for the big one, I too have journeyed up a valley or two; rolled in and out, engulfed and been engulfed, just like that fog. As Robert Duvall said to Tommy Lee Jones in the TV miniseries, **Lonesome Dove,** "By God, Woodrow, it's been one helluva party."

With a few of the party's more savory moments captured on the following pages, kindly do me the honor of reading on.

Prologue

Inhospitable Psychobabble

Lay it all at Arlene's feet.

Given the things that go "bump" in a head like mine, I would have come to it on my own, if meant to be and compatible with the remotest of project plans. She knew it too, knew she had to trick me. What a way to treat some poor son-of-a-bitch under the knife!

As clueless as I am to how she pulled it off is exactly how sure I am she did: bribed the "Am Surg" receptionists; enlisted the head nurse, even chatted up the green-dudded honcho himself in pre-op. But someone whispered, *"Book, Book, Book,"* while they worked on me; had to have.

There we had been; poolside on one of those floating Hindenburgs. Seeing me safely through knocking back a couple of margaritas, out came: "Honey, there's something I want to talk to you about. It's serious."

I was pure armchair.

The vasectomy had held, I knew, but suddenly I'd grown fifteen white knuckles. "I haven't said anything for a couple of months now." The topic was old; my grip eased, as if soothed by the intravenous goop that put wheels on this thing to start with. "Have you thought anymore about your pieces, you know, publishing them together, as a book or something?"

The CO2 found its exit, if ill-advised.

She set me up, see: hadn't had a fling with the ship's trainer; refrained from binge-shopping on the duty free deck, not taken a fifth full time job back in the City. That left the real issue, waiting in the temporal lobes for a drug-induced letting down of my guard.

"In morphino veritas"—and *"grandiositas."*

Being highly sensitive to anything related to adrenaline, in recovery I started convulsing. Whatever cc level they shot me up with to stop it set the roller coaster to motion. *Happily* coming around now, I sang like Tweetie Pie, right after dishing something obscene to one of the nurses.

Another round, and off to the big races: I orated like Patrick Henry, given to the liberty—no the *death*—of my braggadocio. Too late to take any of it back now, my *masterpieces,* yet, were coming out as a highly touted volume. Thought-provoking essays, mind you, hilarious, marketable under all kinds of categories, what with the agents and gazetteers dogging my heels.

A crowd of white coats began to gather; I think I even signed a bedside autograph. I'd been had by my own day-tripping subconscious, the lifelong giddiness I demonstrate every fripping time I feel good.

But, "Devils, shit, and pancakes," as they say in Sweden.*

I have no ambition. I write for me, here and there, sorting something out, or just spouting off. Now I had to fill in the gaps, arrange the vignettes to some kind of sequence, and deal with the overlapping. Worse still, it had to make sense! How would I live? People I know won't believe I really wrote these things!

* *Jävlar, skit, och pankaka*

So, yeah, put it on my wife, her and that damnable hospital! Germanic languages call them by the right name: "Sick Houses." No wonder so many people die there. Staph infections, schmaph infections! The real terror should center on one's imagination, therein chemically unleashed, especially one as bizarre as mine always was anyway....

Sky King

A *Paean to the Man, and an Apology*

Before the end of day one at music camp, they had dubbed him, "Sky King," after the popular TV series of the time, totally unaware of the ways in which it was appropriate. "They" was a group of African-American youths, mostly from the St. Louis area. I was there too, not from the St. Louis area, but all eyes and ears.

It was the late 1950s; among the things that defined the age, we felt every degree of its pre-air conditioned condition. Mr. King would sit there in his boxer shorts with the door open and read. He was hall counselor, and responsible for the way we behaved. As it happened, he was also my public school music teacher, father of the girl I puppy-loved since grade school, and a whole lot more.

It is of more than passing importance to know that "Sky King" loved those St. Louis boys, not in the least demonstrated by their having felt comfortable enough with him— in one day no less—to call him that. As with every other youth he knew, Mr. King cared deeply about their future, and would talk at length of what lay ahead. It was an era in which a lesser man would not have given so much time of his day. But then, "Sky King" was not just a head above us intellectually; he was ahead of his time as well.

I wouldn't know about his upbringing, but during the college and army days, Mr. King had certainly rubbed shoulders with African-Americans. For me it was a brand new experience. No Blacks chose to live in our little town, and I had never hobnobbed with any anywhere else. The era was just before another Mr. King, one Martin Luther, Jr., began raising our national consciousness—and conscience. I was so ignorant I thought there was a rule forbidding Blacks in our county, that is until an acquaintance of my father who, having apparently learned a thing or two in prison, lambasted me for the notion: "Oh, a rule!" he said.

But then, what would you have expected, coming from a family, members of whom that conveniently glossed over Jesus' Jewish heritage, that in the late 1970s exclaimed over a TV talk show host who kissed a woman "black as the ace of spades straight on the mouth," and declared the new clothes they had brought home, moreover got a good price for, came from a store run by, "these Jews." They were Lebanese I later learned, therefore presumably Muslims or Christians, not that then and there most people knew the difference.

Nor did the fault lie just with my family. Though at home we certainly were not allowed to use the "N" word, it was freely heard around and about. I can even remember a school assembly one November in which the elementary principal—a woman about six feet, four inches tall—gave a speech on the subject of things for which to be thankful: being white was one of them. Mr. King, certain to have been present at that assembly, could not have approved.

As much as anything else, Mr. King had a keen appreciation of humor, and the aforementioned St. Louis kids took full advantage. One of the stories he told over and again was that of sitting at his dormitory desk one evening when all the temporary residents started sauntering in, aimlessly accommodating themselves about his room. To be sure they were welcome; counseling them was part of Mr. King's job, and everyone knew the door was truly always open. But after a while it started getting just a tad crowded in that little cubicle, and our floor counselor grew concerned that some would have to sit on that same floor, apparently needing advice all at once. Putting his magazine down, though, Mr. King's unflappable response was, "Boys, how are you?"

What later came to light was that the African-American kids had gone around to all the others, saying, "Meetin' in 'Sky King room in ten minutes and he say yo' ass better be there!" Like everyone else, I obeyed, but had quite a laugh when the truth finally "outted."

I have heard Mr. King's daughter describe some of her own boys as being like him in that they could do almost anything, and that although their grandfather's profession for years had been music teaching, music just might have been what he did least well. The proverbial jack-of-all-trades, he was master of several.

In World War II, Mr. King had flown B-29s and, when it came to aviation, really knew his stuff. The high school course he voluntarily taught in aviation was one of the best I ever took anywhere; he sat there and winged, no pun intended, the whole course off the top of his head. He devoured anything in print, knew electronics and broadcasting, had manual skills, and, in the eleventh hour one year, stepped in as high school principal. Considering what he was to do with the second half of his life, I guess that bug bit him deeply enough to keep itching.

Not that he was any slouch musician, understand, or innovator. Mr. King got funding for and founded a darned good high school drum an bugle corps when most people had no idea what it even was, the alumni of which to this day march in parades. As a seventh grade trombone player on the front row of his regular marching band who kept swinging out on turns and causing the whole line behind him to do the same, I, said Mr. King, was in danger of having a clarinet clunked in my hands so that I could strut my wares in the rear; I would say he needed bodies too much to kick me out altogether.

Curiously, it wasn't long after, that, in the local Christmas parade, I did strut my wares toward the (and *my*) rear, substituting for a sick bass drummer. The woolen pants of our new uniforms (that Mr. King and we baked a lot of cookies raising money for), those pants, I say, were apparently not accustomed to such rubbing and banging from a surrogate; they came down in the middle of the parade and had to be held up by the *clarinet* player marching behind me, and for the rest of the event.

At high school basketball games, I later had to conduct the pep band because Mr. King was off doing something else he either was expected to do as part of his job description, or for which he was simply indispensable.

A large but graceful man with a mostly bald head, he looked not unlike (fittingly, since the name was "King," and he was known to puff on stogies) the picture on a King Edward cigar box. I once saw him- effortlessly- fling a basketball that had bounced into the stands all the way to the goal; what's more, the darned thing almost went in. The call letters for the radio station he started up were "KBHS." My brother, who helped him run

it, said it stood for "King's Bald Head Shines." I never knew if it was true, nor was I brave enough to ask.

But, if it existed, Mr. King was interested in it.

Shortly after his daughter—and I—graduated from high school, he went back to school full time himself, earning his doctorate and becoming no less than Assistant Commissioner of Education for the state of Missouri. Oddly enough, we were all students of the same university at the same time. I had a wonderful relationship with his adorable wife, with whom I had worked at the radio/TV repair shop.

The two of them supported me in what I did, came to my performances in a variety of venues over the years and were, I believe, proud.

Why, then, I ignored them, them of all people, once we went our separate geographical ways, I have little idea. Maybe it was shame that they would find out certain facts about me, over which I'd have to look them in some future eye. I have pondered it again and again, especially since I was known to communicate with other former mentors, people just like Mr. King, whom I wanted to thank.

So why then, not at least a letter? And why, oh why, not an invitation to a certain banquet—to him who was alive, well, and living just down the road—at The University of Missouri when I was presented with a distinguished dormer student award? The only reason I can think of was that I was distracted. Upon learning I was to receive the award, I immediately envisioned my main voice teacher, under whom I had studied more recently than Mr. King, and my father, who had encouraged me to go into music, being there. They both died the meantime, and afterward I apparently just didn't think. In fact, I didn't invite anyone, and for that am truly, truly sorry.

What a perfect place is the sky for one Richard L. "Sky" King. I know that he is up there flying around somewhere, and that he perceives all I think and do, have done and said, and probably will continue to do; that for which, I might add, I am not exactly comfortable. But even though he now knows I am the one that spilled mustard all over the front of band uniform number thirty-six and failed the aviation written test a second time, there is yet something I can do to help make up for the much greater *faux pas*.

If ever I should publish a book, Mr. King, as if he were on personal loan from God, will occupy a prime position, at a guaranteed and fixed rate of interest. Greatly in his debt, my due diligence and title abstract have yielded his official home and place: he is "Sky King," King of the Sky, and a Whole Lot More.

Around The Block In Eighty Days

"Kathy, you little bastard," I hurled at my sister from the back seat, not knowing the gender of the word, much less the meaning.

The praying-together family of five had piled into a borrowed car, taken a left-hand turn out of the driveway, then a right one onto the highway, not quite of my dreams, but my first journey outside the state. It was huge.

Hearing that outburst, however, my father swerved to a second right turn, then a third, and, followed by a yet another, deposited us exactly whence we came. Thus was the trip to Northern Arkansas summarily canceled, not to be rescheduled for about three months, or more exactly, eighty days.

Underscored by the almost rehearsed fluidity my dad made those turns with, to say nothing of my astonishment that not a single word was said to me once back inside the house, I had my first inkling of not having exactly proceeded from a nomadic tribe.

No wonder, then, I was in my upper class years before laying eyes on the likes of any state more than one beyond my home one. From whirlwind trips around the block a few hundred times, to such exotic destinations as Oklahoma and Iowa with The University of Missouri Marching Mizzou, a life that included the educational perks of travel did finally commence.

Not that I hadn't excelled in the more locally confined rigors. With such mapped-out shackles, especially those that said you only traveled somewhere outside church on Sunday if half dead, you can bet I did, for instance, know my Bible, as well as the consequences of not living up to what it said.

Miss Booth, my main high school English teacher, would routinely call on me in class when fishing for a Biblical quote, though once acknowledged that I was not quite the Old and New Testament scholar my brother was.

I can kinesthetically recall marks left on my buttocks from having referred to my impending baptism as getting "dunked." Clearly I was reading the funny papers at the time of utterance. Down deep it was obvious that no baptism was a true baptism if you were not put clean under the H2O. How else were you going to wash away your sins? Never mind that Jesus himself did not go around doing that sort of thing to other people. In spiritual home schooling, if God was not in certain details, you didn't sweat them.

And if not soaked through with that particular lesson of spiritual rebirth already, I got it real fast when, taking in one of the Cecil B. De Mille extravaganzas with my parents, we witnessed "John The Baptist" come face to face with Jesus in the middle of some rivulet, and have the utter audacity—with all that water around—to sprinkle him! De Mille should have been strung up by the two little things camouflaged by any normally unexcited penis and- conversation over the next two decades being evidence- my mother never did get over it.

And yet, I do just believe that that upbringing is one I would not trade, my military initiation to Jacques Cousteau's, "How To Drown In A Baptistery In Six Easy Lessons," notwithstanding.

God knows my mother did everything she could to raise me right. I know, for instance, how much higher my stomach is in my body than my lower intestines, the difference between toilet paper and Kleenex and which goes in the commode without clogging it, how long it takes you to develop lifelong sinus problems traipsing out bareheaded if you washed your hair within the last two months, which side of a girl to walk on, where to locate the light when you read lest you go blind, what case pronoun a preposition takes, and the importance of having clean underwear on at all times, in case, of some fine afternoon, you decide to get yourself killed! *None* of my wives and few of my friends ever knew these things!

*

Surely I am one of the last survivors to freely roam his hometown with a freely roaming pack of dogs trailing behind. Doing so, I was never far from the country and, as a result, absorbed basic common sense along "with." My friends and in-laws read like Danielle Steel novels giving excuses for not sullying (or boring) their children, bringing them by my farm, when otherwise traveling the world over, they deposit their contrails onto that same piece of ground. Whatever (they think) would the kids do, not being plugged in every minute?

Take me and mine.

Growing up, I did all the regular, character-building things: stuck bubblegum under half the seats I ever sat on, watched old winos guzzle their juice in an alley and drizzle it back out like a water gun running low, built a tree house on the edge of town I burned down with a chimney-less indoor fire, shot a cat, traded my piano lessons for ball practice, practically blew my hand off with a Roman candle, led a Guernsey heifer into my front yard to sleep with in a tent, pissed out my second floor window in the middle of the night right above my parents' bedroom, got in trouble with the law for throwing rocks at a bunch of old junk cars, learned how much room there is on the ball team for crybabies when I let go of a few tears to my dad after missing a fly ball, told a friend's dad I wish he were my dad in *front* of my dad, was crazy insane to see any vagina that didn't belong to my little sister, got the scoop on the birds and bees from a friend when I found a diaphragm in his parents' medicine cabinet, and won a baby contest.

Together with a friend, I put three cherry bombs, stuck up lighted cigarettes of differing lengths, under another friend's window one Fourth of July night and went over to the ballpark bleachers to hear them go off. How can a kid be a kid in this Montessori-gone-nuts-ultra-stimulated existence we have now when distances for family outings are measured, not in miles or hours, but Game Boys and CDs?

*

Some of the thrust and dust of my illustrious childhood settled in the vicinity of a makeshift carpenter's studio, not that I was all that good at that sort of thing. My real talent lay in gardening, if in great measure due to the soil composition of our back yard. Though the middle of town, it had been a chicken pen before we moved in. The nitrogen in that ground would have burned up a rain forest, but for growing vegetables was like the precursor to Miracle Grow. I won a prize at the county fair for my tomatoes, the monstrous things having been unsuckered, unmulched, unwatered, and unweeded. Plus, some old coot gave me a secret weapon: "Soak 'em in sugar 'fore puttin' 'm innuh hole."

But, hell, no wonder we're so screwed up today. For the above P. Allen Smith* tomato words, my spell checker suggests, "unscrewed" for "unsuckered," "unmatched" for "unmulched," "unaltered" for "unwatered" and "unwedded" for "unweeded!" What's the world coming to?

Of course, when I started college I *was* pretty ignorant in a bunch of other ways. My freshman class schedule consisted of registered ones five days a week, and impromptu sessions on the real subjects of life in the dorm at night and on the weekends.

And why not? Had it not been more than a year or two since I did things like, on a pleasant summer's evening in which we invited my brother's "nice-family" girlfriend over after church, announce the baby kittens we went outside to peek at were, "suckin' tits?" "Oh, Gary! Nursing!" my father rejoined.

That same father would sometimes let me know how I was looking in other venues too: "Hello, Ugly," he'd say and laugh real big when I'd walk up. Believing it, I spoiled every family portrait we ever

*Gardening professional, author, and TV figure

had made, which-considering my dad was a photographer- meant a lifetime of them, with the stupid faces I'd make. To this day I

To be sure, though, there was always time for other artistic pursuits in that mostly photogenic little family. At get-togethers with our relatives, for instance, we'd always have a hymn-sing around the piano and electric organ before heading home. More formally, my brother got the voice lessons and I the trombone and tuba.

The latter sounds like that country song, "She Got the Goldmine, I Got the Shaft," but wasn't really that way. I had the distinction of being one of the few professional singers I ever knew that could count and learn music. Of course, my college brass teachers helped too: "I'll give you a hint, Dipshit: what was Basie's first name?" They don't give that kind of college instruction nowadays.

Slowly, though, people began to get the idea I could sing.

My dad had a voice like a lumber mill saw and I took up that same splinter, struggling for years trying to give it more the character of a band saw. Why else, not being a natural academician, would I have finished the coursework for a Doctorate in Voice, but that I had run out of degrees and still not learned to sing like a pro?

Still, something had hinted at it early on. At bus outings to the Boys Club, the kids would whistle and catcall when anyone but me dared stand up and hold forth. When I did, they were just quiet.

And I had other indictments: said the local district attorney, "One can enjoy the music just watching young Kendall." When the tune went up, so did my head like a bobble-head doll; likewise into my sternum for what were the depths of an apparently beautiful boy soprano.

In the same auditorium (gymnasium, really) where I sang and conducted with my forehead, played second-string basketball, picked up the prize for my tomatoes, and lost the prince charming contest to a creep, there had also been a carnival box supper. When the bidding started at fifty cents for the box belonging to the girl I had a crush on, I jumped up and shouted: "Three dollars and twenty-one cents!" Everyone laughed, and had not the heart to bid against me. But how could the poor girl go for me? She was the daughter of a local automobile dealership owner, and there I was, an ignorant little shrimp from a family that didn't even own a car.

Wheel-worthy or not, I eventually made it beyond the *Missouri Breaks*. Some of those first *fine turnings* were compliments of the university choir, performing for a week at the 1964 New York World's Fair. The virgin eyes and ears were open, and I could fill another book with the impressions, captured in a diary that years later flabbergasted me to read.

From time to time I try to recapture that innocence. I get out of the downtown #1 local subway, and mosey past the Holiday Inn on West 57th Street where we made fun of the waitresses' pronunciation of, "cwoffee." Strolling by—at least other than when on my way to Roosevelt Hospital for surgery—I try to prove one could ever have been so young and dumb, so hale, hearty and smarty. I have not come up with the evidence.

Clearing the Big City hurdle, I leapt into another of life's travelogues: my first jet ride, also the maiden one to Europe. Highlights from the Little Bible Boy's initial romp over the pond were, 1) exclaiming, as we came wheels down at Heathrow Airport, that they had grass just like we did, 2) keeping my nose stuck in a cheap mystery during a trip through the staggeringly beautiful Norwegian *Fjords*, and 3) the first time in my life confronted by someone who didn't address me in English, raising my right hand like a good Native American and offering up: "Non-Speak!"

But things would look up. Around the world in another eighty days, or years, and I might act like I had "been there" before. It was time; I had made a ton of mistakes, leaving my parents proud but wondering if their baby hadn't been switched in the hospital, or brought home by some wayward stork with the bird flu. Not just being a "trip" myself, I had *made* a couple and wanted more.

And the girl with the box supper? She finally came around. At our twentieth class reunion, her voice went up about an octave when she saw me, but I wished I had my three bucks back. Most of the ones, in fact, that I had been in love with at one time or other, now divorced, cackled at how much better looking I was than in high school, and chomped at the bit to get to the star of the evening's entertainment, which I, yes, *I*, brought off in pretty fair fashion, despite the piano accompaniment from my first keyboard teacher.

Instead, I coughed up another three, and put it toward a six-pack. I was driven to the party at a classmate's farm, and spent most of the night sitting under the stars wishing I had a piece of ground of my own. At length it was I just sat there, contemplating life's circumnavigations and other mysteries, including, very much, my very *own* TRUE NATURE.

With Tibor Once More

Preface

It was no worse than all the other atrocities of the time; only it seems so since I personally knew HIM. With ONE so talented, so learned, so principled, so accomplished, so disciplined, and for the most part so true, the pain lingers that it all should have ended the way it did.

My understanding of the story is part personal experience, part conveyance, part hearsay, and part piecing together over time. Still, I present it as fact, owing to the reliability of my sources, and the compatibility with my own impressions.

No written collection of my life could be remotely complete without something of HIM who taught me so much. The whole world is what it would be worth to be able to sit down once more with HIM, look across a table, pitting (HIS frequent word) what my own years have brought to that same surface. Alas, it is too late, and in so many modes....

*

HIS fiancée was dark-featured, beautiful, and deeply loved, offering no less, yet no more, candidacy for extermination than all the others. We can't begin to know the extent of it.

Escaping the same goose-stepping fiends, HE then made it to our side of the Atlantic, and by the early 1940s was earning a living conducting, not HIS type of music, but for a handsome Broadway buck. When the voice on the other end of the line offered HIM an assistant conductorship- a glorified name for "coach-" at the Metropolitan Opera, HE took it without hesitation, and for a third of HIS existing salary, therein commencing the uphill slide. HE was said to have been one of the best coaches the MET ever had.

Max Rudolf, head of conductors at the MET during that period, personally told me that he would admonish HIM for being so Prussian, asking, "Where is the Hungarian in you?" It was there, I have to believe, just buried in someone else's grave.

One of HIS favorite sayings was, "The human voice is one of MY favorite instruments; it's too bad most of them belong to singers."

Also, "It is MY conviction that one should speak his native language perfectly," which HE did, along with several others, including HIS heavily accented English- I always suspected left that way intentionally- about which HE taught me more than almost any other person.

"Singing is stronger than speaking!" he would yell from the orchestra pit when someone shouted a note instead of sing it. And you were smart to duck if you held a note longer than someone else the way "fifth rate Italian" singers did.

When Leontyne Price came to Indiana University the second time to perform, they asked if she would do so with the school's select orchestra. She answered in the affirmative, but only if He conducted. Amidst a sea of compliments, HIS only criticism of her was that she answered in the negative his letter asking her to "challenge her audience" with something other than the opera aria program she had selected. School performances of works, such as the Mozart and Verdi operas over which he presided, were better than any I have heard since.

Arrested for drunken driving in Bloomington, Indiana the paper indicated HE could have got off more easily except for the added charge of insulting an officer. HE refused to own a TV, criticized

American cars, feuded openly with other faculty members as if they were students themselves, and was unswerving in his opinion of someone, especially if that someone was a student of a teacher HE didn't like. When one such student approached the orchestra pit before a rehearsal, saying, "Hey, like, what's happenin', Man." You never heard such diatribe about speaking "jive talk" to HIM, him who always addressed students as Mr. and Miss, saying that since he didn't call the students by their first names, he could expect the same from them.

And if the above should be considered faults, he had others as well.

In general, it was HIS way or the highway: the linguist, HE refused to conduct school opera except in the vernacular, which HE would scream must be stage English. HE had little use for ornaments in Baroque music and would not take a conducting student who was not an accomplished pianist. In appearance, a handsome version of Albert Einstein, HE would have none of dance girls' throwing themselves at him at HIM at the MET, saying always, HE was "one-woman man."

If HIS wife, a lovely person who slightly resembled a character from a Dickens novel, came to pick HIM up before rehearsal was over,

HE would search from the pit, find her in the house seats, and wave. Childless, they were devoted to each other. Yet we knew not the extent of the story.

Somewhere, down along the—or between this book's—lines, I will have indicated my obvious lunacy for a taste in mentors. While everyone else went right on hating the hard ones, I usually demonstrated one of my few measures of maturity, feeling that the harder I fell the better I learned, and the more important those lessons would become in retrospect.

HE was always at the top of my mentor list, though I eventually disappointed HIM by my growing rebellious student nature. Having once been HIS pet, the letter from HIM in my university placement file blasted me from "here to there." What HE taught me had been from the moral high ground as much as anywhere else, and I ultimately failed HIM, perhaps because HE seemed to fail me with what was trickling down from those lofty plains.

*

Some fifteen years after I had known and been repeatedly instructed and conducted by HIM, I learned the referred-to greater extent of HIS life's story, and why HE therefore thrust HIS front-engineless Carmenghia front end into a large tree somewhere near Bloomington.

It was rumored, from about the middle of my last year at the school, that an attractive co-ed had made a strong and greatly insistent play for HIM, eventually, when HIS wife was out of town, becoming irresistible. It had commenced with something as innocuous as an in-class performance by the young woman, who, when HE expressed something to the effect that she had sung a phrase flat, answered that she hadn't known she was flat; responded THE MAESTRO, "No, my dear; you are not flat, your singing is." Her saucy response was to the effect that she didn't know HE cared.

That HIS remorse was great at having admitted her to HIS house, not living up to HIS considerable principles, was understandable; that HE wouldn't let her in the next time, all the more so. But sounding off at the top of her "singerly" lungs from his front porch proved also too much to resist, and a second admittance established the liaison forever, if not for good.

In near disbelief, I saw evidence of the rumors around me. And on it went, after I had moved to Philadelphia, culminating in an early morning confrontation between the two principle females, when HE had taken ill during a morning walk, from all reports alcohol- related. The confrontation was, understandably, not a pretty sight. But then, when HIS wife succumbed to brain cancer a relatively short time later, HE apparently chose to join her. Yet we knew not the extent of why.

*

HE had not been admitted to our country easily. A young American woman was found, sight unseen, for HIM to marry, which, in those days, rather automatically resulted in "citizenship". She wasn't pretty, presumably not loved, no candidate for extermination, and true blue. In return, HE stuck to her like Epoxy, which became the very glue that held HIM together for lo, those many years as well.

Early in the marriage, HE HIMSELF said that they had had trouble, and to the extent that HE had to ask HIMSELF if HE wanted to be with "this woman" or not. Responding to HIS own question with the emphatic words, "Hell, yes," HE commenced the easier to get along with, and faithful epoch. But to a man in HIS fifties with HIS particular life's story, one subsequent young co-ed proved endlessly, as well as finally, too persistent.

Almost a decade after HIS demise, I happened to attend a party in New York City. It was hosted by the young woman in question, since moved to the Upper West Side of Manhattan. Entering the front door, the first thing I saw was an eight-by-ten glossy photo of HIM, resting on her bookcase. I could scarcely function socially for the rest of the evening from the thoughts that were racing though my mind. Not the least of the thoughts was that after all those years, she was still with HIM, constituting yet another true blue woman, now in an open and relaxed- if lonely- place.

The university personnel HE left the MET to teach with pretty much hated HIM both during HIS life, and since HIS death. HIS faults notwithstanding that school—like most others I know since—has gone through periods of mere "shadowiness" of its former glory. Had it HIS standards and principles amidst the tsunami of artistic laxity we ubiquitously have today, it would be the crowning institution of the land. But the powers that be, that were, and that *not* be, fail to see past their rationalizing noses, thus never comprehending the extent of it all.

I learned more from HIM than any other professor, except for my own collegiate voice teacher of many years, with whom HE feuded from time to time, though one of the few he addressed by her first name, and had known since their Met days.

Maybe what I learned from him is why I forever battled stiffness as a performer. I was for years, after all, quite the good boy: to the punctuality fanatic, I was always early. To the fiend for musical dependability, I was exact. In the face of HIS constant crankiness for *legato* in singing, I endeavored to put my notes together as by an atom smasher; and to HIS open and vicious critique of the newly formed Gay Liberation Front, I always liked girls.

Once I had gained HIS confidence, HE normally requested me for productions HE conducted, saying, "I am naturally inclined toward people not plagued by musical difficulties." If I messed up in rehearsal, HE would only say, "Once more, please," when to others HE would have screamed.

On one occasion when HE knew I had been required to do more than what even HE thought one could handle, and basically faked my way through a piano ensemble rehearsal with HIM, HE said nothing until, running into me the next day, with a slightly sardonic nod of his head, quipped only: "Well, now we know you can *"rrreadd"* music.

In a mid-week stage brush-up rehearsal for a performance to be given on the weekend, HE once flattered me by stopping and, in front of the entire cast and chorus, asked, "Mr. Kendall, this ensemble was not together in the last performance; I wonder if you could tell me why?" Without missing a beat, I replied: "Mr. Schuba rushes." Responded THE MAESTRO, "The devil take him."

In a performance a few weeks later of the same work for which the Indianapolis Symphony provided the orchestra, the so-called concertmaster, as HE called him, musically entered during an empty two-beat spot before my own solo entrance, bringing the entire orchestra with him. Speaking of the incident a few days later, HE said only, "Well, somewhere in the back of my mind I knew I did not have to worry about you."

But, toward the end of my student days, things began to erode. I was singing the role of "Don Basilio" in an out-of-town presentation of Rossini's *The Barber of Seville*. This performance was conducted by a graduate student and, as such, had to be evaluated by a member of the conducting faculty. I had never known HIM to take such an assignment, but, since the "Rosina" for that particular performance was HIS girlfriend, HE drove all the way to do the grading. Backstage after the performance, HE met me in a crowd of people, saying that all through the performance HE had thought that it was my cover, a young man named John Paul—a tall, but at the time, less accomplished bass-baritone than I—singing the part instead of me.

Somehow I knew it meant my one-woman-man maestro had had his mind on other things. With his concubine standing at HIS side, I blurted it out, "Shit," leaving HIS eyebrows plastered against his striking gray hairline as I made my way back to the dressing room. It ushered in the season of our discontent, and to this day and no matter what my reasons, I wish I had not said and done it.

Most of what HE taught me was imbued with the same rigidity that led to HIS unhappy life and early end, not that I blame HIM, looking back. That legacy has been of more value than my courses, my books, my other coaches and conductors, my years-long experience of varying types, and more even than anything which I have had to *un*learn. Ergo, my gratitude for it, and for HIM, is as it has always been: unending, and only HIS untimely death prevented my telling HIM the extent of it.

From Valhall-arious to Missile-aneous

A funny thing happened on the way to my career. In fact it kept on happening, even when I didn't want it to. Looking back, that side of my performing life is the one I think of most fondly.

Apparently I came by the chortles honestly. My mother's uncle was comical, especially telling tales of his life as a deputy sheriff in the Oklahoma Territory. Said my great Uncle Jim to one denizen of iniquity, "Mister, if you don't want to see you sweet Jesus right now, drop that shooter and park you hind end on the floor."

In junior high, when our teacher stepped out and the kids were raising hell, I was always the one that got caught. In other, more innocuous circumstances, such as Boy Scout outings, I prognosticated a pretty solid future as a stand-up comic.

An opera apprentice at the Chautauqua, NY Institute in 1969, I cracked some off-color joke backstage just before we choristers were to let lose a rowdy song in *The Student Prince*. It was rowdy all right. At the time that chorus master Robert Spillman gave the downbeat, we were laughing too hard to sing. Spillman, ever the professional, continued to beat time for the entire piece to either total silence or occasional outbursts resembling alley cats in the act of getting pregnant. At the end of the supposedly *rousing* chorale, he quipped, "Thank you, gentlemen, for your usual fine job," and walked away. Thirty years later, when he and I were faculty colleagues at the Aspen Music School, I reminded him of the incident. After all that time, there were still no chortles issuing forth from him. .

Of course, there is nothing in heaven or on earth funnier than that which is not meant to be so, unless it is something not meant to be that way *onstage*!

My first rendering of the bass solos in Haydn's great oratorio, **The Creation,** took place in a cow palace in Madison, Wisconsin. The floor, covered with sawdust, was the very spot where various moo-moos had been coaxed about and judged for their ham-hock content during county fair-like events. For the Haydn, we did it differently. A tall, temporary stage was erected, with folding chairs placed about the former hoof prints for the audience to judge our ham-hock content from about five feet below.

Atop the center of the arena was a set of old fashioned loud speakers, in this case the roost for a flock of sparrows that, like all serious music lovers, sat noiselessly; that is, until I finished the big recitative depicting God's creation of all great and small creatures. Suddenly, they chirped like crazy, as if applauding!

At the time I was still bouncing between the trombone and singing, the University of Missouri Music Department had an all-school ensemble called, "Collegium Musicum," to my knowledge the first of its kind in the 20th century. The Collegium would twice yearly present music from another epoch, possibly another solar system, or so it sounded. These educational marathons also lasted about as long as the epoch in which they were written, featuring oldies-but-not-goodies from about the time Adam and Eve were small children.

The concerts always attracted puzzlingly large audiences, most of which wandered over from other, more progressive centers of campus learning. Ninety percent of the music department was, after all, on the stage.

The "Sackbut," aptly called, was the name of the Renaissance trombone. In Collegium, making me a "Sackbut" player, which eliciting a number of wisecracks in and of itself.

The founder of the "Collegium Musicum" was—who else?—the faculty musicologist, one Dr. Andrew C. Minor, whom we lovingly referred to as Dr. Andrew E-flat Major.* At least once every concert, some composer's *magnum minus* would fall irrevocably apart and Dr. Minor would halt the Mixolydian** proceedings with a grand cutoff, after which we would try once more.

Such things tended to be funny. In fact, the most difficult thing about Collegium in general was keeping a straight face, especially hearing some of the instruments, such as the "Krummhorn" and the "Serpent." Dr. Minor, God bless him, had obviously been in contact with the Ghost of Music Past to come up with these dusty-and-rusty-plowshares-beat-into-instruments-of-musical-destruction, which he pleadingly passed out to the teachers and students of their modern versions.

We sackbut players had an advantage: a physical workout while playing. The slides that determined musical pitch had been chemically fused since the pre-WD Forty-days of Johannes Ockeghem (ca.1430-

---

* E-flat major and c minor are relative, therefore closely related, musical keys
** A musical mode. Modes were precursors to our modern musical keys, of which "major" and" minor" are the two that have survived

1495), and were well nigh impossible to move. After a few embouchure bruises and tooth chips, we more resembled sacked-quarterbacks.

In case you have ever tried, you know it is very difficult to sing while either laughing or crying. In Mexico, just before standing up to sing in a rehearsal of the Mozart *Requiem*, one of my colleagues asked me what my solo line, "Tuba Mirum Spargens Sonum" meant. Without missing a beat on the way to my feet, I replied, "There's asparagus sounding in my tuba." Our vocal quartet didn't, however, sound for the next couple of pages.

Fully staged opera contains even greater possibilities for unintentional hilarity, owing to the presence of visual treasures, as well as musical. Indeed some of the funniest things that I ever saw or heard of happened in connection with opera.

One of my students told me of a friend who had been a spear-carrier for a production of Richard Strauss' **Salome** and, as such, was directed to be the first human being to see the separated head of "John The Baptist." As is often the case, the prop crew had not readied the properly painted version of said object of decapitation until the first actual performance and, when completed, was made to look real from the audience, as opposed to up close. At that highly dramatic moment on opening night, the young man's inexperienced thespian response was to burst out laughing.

Murphy's Law of Opera is: *If anything ever goes wrong onstage, the next sung line provides a perfect comment on the mishap,* making comic opera infinitely funnier than what the librettist and composer could have come up with, and what was not supposed to be funny at all, *very* funny indeed.

The referred-to summer in Chautauqua, New York contained a season-long host of theatrical disasters. To wit for one of them, a low male voice singer in the apprentice program was a notably obnoxious human being by the name of Harry, who, though possessing a fine native vocal instrument had yet to evince signs of being a musical creature, or a bright one.

The show was **La Bohême**. For one of the nights in question, the audience had been primed from the first curtain. One of Lake Chautauqua's famous bats had made its way into the auditorium and flown around the stage during act one, offering strange comments on what the principal singers were saying to each other. Their gestures, as they fought off the dive-bomber, made the production look like some kind of S&M conception, whereby the characters of "Mimí" and "Rodolfo" were trying to knock each other silly as they professed their sudden undying love. These contrasting actions warmed up the audience really well.

Enter the chorus at the top of act three. You may know how it goes in English: short repeated shouts of, "Holá! Wake up there! Wake up there." The text then describes the cold, snowy conditions, in our case visually enhanced by bits of squeezably soft Chairmen tissue paper, the source of which was this giant, hula-dancing contraption hoisted high above the faintly lit stage.

Fittingly, bathroom commodes are not the only things in which tissue gets clogged. As if demonstrating yet another weather forecast that missed, our snow machine began to dwindle, and soon was putting out absolutely nothing. Following some moments of this curious visible and textual contradiction, the machine came most definitely unclogged, depositing a glob the size of a small polar bear about the central portion of Harry's head.

The next sung line from the chorus, which came immediately, was

"Look how it's snowing!" The audience "dissolved," thereby audibly obliterating "Mimí's" subsequent poignant entrance, and leaving anyone who didn't know the opera to wonder what some chick with bronchitis was doing standing in the dark and dank recesses of the stage.

But performers are human too. No matter how much they get into their roles, they're only playacting up there, and amusing things don't escape their attention either. If something goes awry, it is not always easy for them to maintain control, despite being made-up and fully costumed, so that what was stated at the outset of this chapter is perhaps most true of them, namely that the more you shouldn't laugh the more you need to.

The year before the Chautauqua Institute summer, I had been an apprentice with the Santa Fe Opera. We were doing Henze's aboriginal story-based opera, *The Bassarids,* for which we Act Two chorus members were required to be unclothed, except for some artificial plant-like growths protruding from the tops of our heads and *genitalia aboriginia.*

The stage set consisted of two quite large metal ramps, originating low and narrow upstage, widening upward as they branched downstage. Camouflaging the ramps were great clumps of "underbrush," which enabled us to look out from underneath as if we were about to say, "Boo!"

Chorus master Martin Smith- in his street clothes- also hid amongst the dense dollops of *faux* foliage, giving us the quite difficult musical cues by means of a sort of "kissing" noise. We knew Martin fairly well by that point in the summer and thought it appropriate. The dissonant music tickled us youngsters anyway, our getups more, and, given Martin's effeminate manner—now punctuated by these seemingly origin-less puckering—most of all; that is, until one of our members succumbed to a touch of flatulence.

I for one do not find jokes on scatological topics funny. At that particular time, however, a heart attack would have been amusing, especially since the episode occurred at the quietest moment of the entire opera. To be exact, it was during a "grand pause," a point in which *no sound whatsoever* was to emanate from the orchestra pit, stage, or body part.

We choristers found this occurrence tickling. In fact, we found it real tickling, so that the more we attempted to be serious young professionals, the more difficult it was to control our inner convulsions over this short but pungent addition to the score.

Once the orchestra and principals began again with the obtuse story tension, so proceeded that very quality amongst our ranks. Soon what had been a minor jocular hiss increased to the point that the branching ramps on which we precariously crouched appeared to be taking on the appearance of a slight earth tremor.

Next, they commenced to shake, eerily so, back and forth waving in front of the Sangre de Cristo mountain chain out the back of the stage, while we, noticing the effect, found more gleeful still the awareness that we were in danger. We were, in fact, so giddy that nothing mattered; dying itself was not going to disturb the party, as we desperately tried to get hold of ourselves enough to portray our little jungle personas.

As our merriment level reached a mild stage roar, the scene mercifully came to a sudden close, with the lights falling to an immediate blackout.

We young professionals "slunk" down our ramps, took off in a dead run for the acoustical insulation of the dressing area, fell into a huge pile and gave vent to the loudest belly guffaws our incipient operatic instruments could muster. A few moments more onstage and we would have erupted into a sidesplitting heap of mechanical and carnal wreckage, banning us from operatic stages for the rest of our professional lives.

But then, Santa Fe in 1968 always seemed "snake bit." The original opera house had burned down after at the end of the previous season, while the newly constructed substitute was technically still unfinished as the season of my first apprenticeship began. Earlier in the season, Maralin Niska, and most interesting diva in her best moments, had recently given us a truly consumptive "Violetta."*

In an onstage thespian flurry over her feelings for the young "Alfredo," she inadvertently sucked down some liquid left behind by a chorister in one of the plastic champagne glasses used for props. Miss Niska coughed and hacked; she spoke, moaned, gagged and chortled

---

*In Verdi's opera, *La Traviata,* the heroine, "Violetta," dies of tuberculosis, referred to, especially in earlier times, as consumption.

her way through *Ah, forse lui,* until it truly sounded like the well-known métier paraphrase, "Ah, Force Me, Louie."

This bit of stage work was quite something for us kids to take in from the wings, though not nearly so educational as the Vesuvial eruption that was Madame Niska's exit from what was supposed to have been her big aria, as we all stood there taking it in.

I have come to believe that the events of those two apprentice summers set off a chain reaction of onstage mishaps that followed me around the rest of my musical life. While a student at Indiana University not long after, I was performing the role of "Don Alfonso" in Mozart's *Così fan tutte.* The score contains some of Mozart's most beautiful and, for once, does not center around a storyline curse, though in every other way did seem so to be so thwarted.

That school year, I had been cast in every opera that famously operatic music school had mounted, plus a couple of others outside the school. Since it was the quickest I had ever prepared a role, I was not my usual musically solid self and had asked the tenor to help make sure I came on stage for a specific entrance that I kept tending to forget.

In rehearsals, he never once thought to oblige me, but for

opening night had it utmost in his mind, even as I had remembered perfectly and was already on stage when he sought to remind me. When the young man didn't see me backstage he panicked and went looking for me in the dressing area, quite so that everyone onstage, as well as the audience, was naturally looking for *him.*

Well, we waited, then waited some more. We waited for what seemed an eternity. This part of the opera was depicted in what is called *secco* recitative, so that one singer cannot go on without the other singer's line, in this case, the tenor's, but also because the conductor—doubling as the harpsichordist—had to fill in at the keyboard with small improvisations while we principals followed suit with muggings and superfluous gestures—all to the accompaniment of the back stage microphone desperately paging the tenor.

Finally came the heavy footfalls, followed by a series of crashes. Our missing colleague burst suddenly on the scene through the upstage center door, tripping as he did so and almost falling onto his face as he entered. And what was this next line we had all been waiting for? It was, *naturally,* "What now?!" The audience "lost it" while the rest of us held on the best we could.

But even rehearsals can be comedy shows.

Fifteen years after the *Creation* performance, I was back in Madison for a production of Verdi's **Aida**, for which I was cast in the role of the high priest, "Ramfis."

The man singing the smaller role of the "King" was a local construction boss from Milwaukee and had the most awesome bass voice that I to this day have ever heard. The sound this man made was absolutely otherworldly. Every night that he sang, all of us imported New York professionals would stand there with our mouths open, taking in this "phenom."

But one night our amazing "King" was ill and had stayed home. His cover, however, an even more local guy, stepped in for him. This delightful denizen measured about three feet tall by three feet wide, and was an Episcopalian minister. Before rehearsal we were repeatedly warned by the director not to laugh when he sang, which was a little insulting to us consummate professionals, who would never think to do such a thing.

At the point in the opera that the "King" commenced singing, all other principals on stage were directed to be lined up "company front" style across the front edge of the stage, directly above the orchestra pit and facing the audience, while the stage hands changed the scenery behind the closed curtain.

Having been accustomed to hearing "The King's" opening lines bellowed like an amplified pregnant water buffalo at a rock concert, you can imagine our reaction when this little rector turned out to sound like "Popeye's" baby brother entertaining the troops at his own castration ceremony.

Too, this little guy had learned his part by rote from a recording, and clicked off the words and notes like a Teletype machine, one sixteenth-note of which the conductor couldn't have altered with a jackhammer.

Well, we consummate professionals began to laugh. The "Kingly" contrast between these two principals would have caused the pope himself to send peals up to the gargoyles during a solemn *Requiem Mass* at St. Peters. We laughed and we laughed some more, trying, *naturally,* all the time not to. We laughed aloud and "blew" every single one of our cues, nearly falling face forward onto the brass and woodwind players. Most of us were from the same professional artist management firm in New York, and would often perform together in the future. When we did, we relived the incident, agreeing that it was the single most hysterical theatrical moment we would in five lifetimes witness on an opera stage.

At about the time my perennial student days at Indiana University had appeared to be drawing to a close, the IU Opera Theater was producing Wagner's **Die Walküre.** I myself was supposed to have sung the part of "Hunding" but through some rebellious student act, refused.

Dr. D. Ralph Appleman of the Indiana University voice faculty was cast in the role of "Wotan." Dr. Appleman, my teacher for one year, was an interesting fellow, renowned for his scholarly pursuits in vocal science, his absent mindedness, his gentlemanly but sticky-fingered ways with the coeds, his prodigious *basso cantante* voice, and, perhaps most of all, his daring acrobatic stage stunts. He was famous, for instance, for falling head first down a flight of stairs at the end of "Boris Goudonov's" last monologue, eventually netting him a broken collarbone.

By the time of the *Walküre* production, Dr. Appleman, never the most musically secure, was already in his mid-sixties and didn't see so well, especially without his glasses. In any number of opera world's productions *since* the 1960's, he would have been perfectly well equipped wearing a monocle and a top hat. But for this more standard conception, "Wotan" actually looked like "Wotan," and—being a "god," after all—shouldn't logically being seen as needing any correction to his one eye. But for once, the type of stage production Wagner envisioned was unfortunate.

The *Walküre* "Wotan" role is extensive and demanding. It had taken Dr. Appleman quite a long time to learn it, but things were apparently not going badly in rehearsals. I, myself, was interested in Wagner and, for one of the final dress rehearsals, sat in the back of the main floor, taking in everything I could.

At the opening of the second act stood a sort of skeletal, abstract tree, positioned directly at the foot of the stairway where "Wotan" was to make his entrance, presumably from Valhalla. As he entered, I noticed that Dr. Appleman's "Wotan" was moving slowly, even sadly, down the stairs, as if anticipating the sort of dejection he sinks into later, after his wife works him over for a good hour and a half. In this case, I just assumed that, with his bad eyesight, Dr. Appleman was placing his steps so as not to trip.

Indeed he was.

The aforementioned tree was no great work of stage art. In fact, it looked just a little funny standing there by itself. However, when Dr. Appleman reached the bottom of the steps and walked straight into one of its lateral limbs, it looked a lot funnier still. Without being there it is impossible to describe how the incident appeared, especially not knowing firsthand just how absent-minded Dr. Appleman could be; to us he looked his normal self, only this time in full makeup and costume, disguised as a tall houseplant.

Plus, knowing him as we did, we half-expected Dr. Appleman to pull some trapeze-like maneuver and were "on the floor" holding our stomachs waiting for a traffic cop to point the principal's way out of the branching gridlock in which Dr. Appleman had wandered.

Meanwhile, in an absolute Typhoon of music and stage contradiction, the orchestra was blistering those inimitable, surging, rhythms that open act two, while Wotan- hung up in more ways than one- was actually remembering his lines for once, instructing

Brünnhilde, who was nowhere near the tree, to go win the battle for "Hunding," though looking more like "Hunding" himself climbing out of his own full-sized tree, which every good Wagnerian knows grows out of his living room floor!

It was opera's new "mad scene," one of the most naturally hilarious things I have ever witnessed, although we never knew if Dr. Appleman had the slightest inkling of the madness he had created in the seating area.

Some music events are laugh-feasts waiting to happen from their inception. One of them, even in today's anything-goes-world, is modern music. In my humble opinion, the comic element is totally justified, since about ninety-eight percent of what is called *avant garde* or "music today," is pure garbage.

Going back to this chapter's central theme, have you ever been in a social company for which something funny must be suppressed? You desperately want to laugh but can't? Then something is said that is only mildly amusing and the room erupts in much stronger laughter than is warranted?

Such is the way performances of modern music can be. Even

though they bought the tickets themselves, most audience members think they're witnessing a bunch of nonsense, and before long one can sense a kind of giddiness in the air. If such an audience ever gets one real thing to laugh at, it can go on and on. And on.

In 1973, I was a finalist in the Montreal International Singing Competition. All contestants had been required to perform parts of what the French Canadians called a *pièce imposé* by native son composer Murray Shaffer. In all honesty, the piece was not bad, though set to hieroglyphic text fragments, obviously unearthed for the occasion. These fragments were a good choice only in that the differing international singers would be at equal disadvantage.

As I recall, we were furnished translations and pronunciation guides, and I for one, really got "into" the assignment. Taking what I had learned from director Dino Yannopolous at the Curtis Institute, I went to work on the missing textual links. I went so far as to work up "A Typical Day in the Life of a Hieroglyphic Man," supplying material, at least in my own head. After all, how was I supposed to interpret something that had no story? The worst thing anyone can say about a performance is that it lacks meaning and is boring. I was being every inch an incipient artist and good boy.

Accordingly, I innocently interpreted one movement in a slightly humorous vein, though immediately returned to a serious mood for the next. The audience caught my humor for the one fragment just fine and responded fetchingly. It meant that I was getting through, and I was pleased. After all, I had spent a lot of time, also money, preparing for the event.

There was, however, a hidden problem. The following referred-to serious movement had not only a few spoken words, but a number of sub-glottal vocal sounds *from the orchestra members* as part of its orchestration! Of course, there was no way I could have known that. Up until the one-and-only orchestra rehearsal that morning, all I had ever heard was a piano reduction; I couldn't change my interpretation at that point. Besides, I never dreamed of what was about to occur.

Keep in mind that all finalists were required to sing movements from the piece that night, which means that the Schaffer took up the entire program. That, in and of itself, was quite an expectation for the most earnest of concertgoers, and by intermission the audience members- starting to wonder if they were having fun yet- hoped for something to put this "imposing" little piece into a context they could relate to.

I gave it to them.

When I put my humorous little touch to the one movement, the good people of the audience over-laughed. Then, concurring that this whole thing was about the biggest pile of dung they too had ever heard, the orchestra members betook themselves of the same means of relief. As if thwarting my attempts to be a serious artist, they now began to execute their sub-glottal utterances with more gusto than they had in rehearsal that morning, and I could feel them behind me, elbowing each other in the side as they grunted. Fortunately, thought I, the next movement was also serious, and everyone would calm down.

But the listeners, concluding that they liked laughing better, decided that for the next movement I was being *mock* serious, and indulged their glee at this bit of irony all the more. The instrumentalists, meanwhile, feeling sure that music could be fun after all, started to chuckle. Ditto the conductor, Franz-Paul Decker, who broke out into grins looking at me, as both the main floor and balcony were setting up for a major Richter Scale rumble.

Curiously, even *I* now began to "get off" on the experience. I thought I finally understood what my teachers always meant when they said, "Enjoy it more!" or, "Go out there and have fun!" True, I was a tad concerned that my serious movements were not being understood. But, what the hell! I was eliciting what every performer strives for, a *response*. Everyone in the house was having a blast- well, except for the composer, who sat in the mezzanine with the competition judges.

The things that I later learned many found to be an improvement to the score now took a pronounced turn for the worse. The wind players began to lose the ability to blow steadily into their instruments. To their professional credit, they put forth a series of intermittent honk-like blasts, at best resembling squawks of wayward overhead foul on their way south, concluding with *subito crescendi* at the end of certain attempted notes.

In response to this particular collision of classical sound, the elasticity of the string players' bow arms now began to fail them, as Maestro Decker, in turn, seemed to convey difficulty with an upright podium posture, imparting much less musical clarity in the movements of his baton. Indeed, my entire performance, to say nothing of my standing in the competition, threatened to come to a shrieking halt.

By the mercy of God, the music was as fragmented as the text and at the moment of the entertainment's highest pitch, my presentation slammed to its conclusion like a guillotine blade.

The place went bonkers, exploding from the house orchestra seats to the very top of the balcony. I had never known success like this. Surely I would win the competition, even if I had scored poorly in previous rounds. The eyes of the other competitors were on me like daggers, the conductor and players like groupies, swamping me with backstage hugs, their words making me out to be the only singer they ever liked.

But the morning papers crucified me. They said I had made fun of the music and that the composer had been gravely insulted. The judges, also affronted, penalized me for the same irreverence. I had been in the running for the top prize before that round of singing, but in the final tabulations was knocked down to a tie for seventh place out of the original fifty performers who had made it into the competition.

Such was my reward for the most thorough preparation of a piece of music that to this day I have ever undertaken (let alone performed), for bestowing on the composer the biggest reception he would ever deserve (let alone receive) and for giving a modern audience the best time it would ever dream of (let alone have).

*

Owing to my student status at the Curtis Institute of Music, I was invited to spend a couple of summers at its sister musical organization at the time, the Marlboro Music Festival. Though never a singer's place, it was an honor to be invited to Marlboro, and was a stimulating summer experience. Many of the participants, running around barely more than kids, went on to have big careers. Of course, I had been told that Marlboro was fun and that it should therefore fit right in with my personality.

I had already come to know the great Rudolf Serkin, director of both the Curtis Institute and Marlboro, well enough to speak to him in the hallways of Curtis. I had known recordings of his before having been invited to Curtis; to me he was little short of a god. Plus he and I ran into each other stepping off the same train in Philadelphia, delighting in discovering that we had performed on opposite ends of Kennedy Center at the same time earlier that evening.

Consistent with his old world elegance, Serkin insisted on taking me home by taxi, and instructed the driver to go to my address first, though quite out of the way. The driver, however, drove to Mr. Serkin's home on Delancy Street. All Serkin did was refuse to get out of the cab, insisting that the driver go on to my apartment across town, then bring him back. It was the most special of moments from the most special of people.

As was the beginning of the Marlboro Music Festival, June 1973.

My family and I arrived in a pouring rain, just as dinner was ending. At Marlboro, things were not fancy. The table cloths were made of paper and I was to learn the hard way that everyone's way of pitching in on cleanup was to wad up the paper table covers and, after throwing them at each other, put them in the trash cans.

When I sat down to scarf up a few remaining morsels, 'WHAP'! something slapped me smack in the back of the head. The object was a missile, wet, and thrown at considerable force from the hands of some dastardly human being with a highly developed set of arms and hands. As it fell to the floor, I could see that the missile was made of the same material that covered the tables. To myself I thought, "Good God! What the hell kind of place is this?" Instinctively, I looked around for the culprit, probably the *brat* that would do such a thing to a new arrival, trying to keep from starving.

From all the stares in his direction, as well as the canary-swallowed look on his face, however, it was clear that the offender had been none other than the ever elegant, super mild-mannered, saintly Rudolf Serkin himself.

Instantly it was transformed to something that thrilled me, and I started to laugh. So welcomed and deeply honored was I to have been whacked by the great man himself that it became something that I will never ever forget, nor fail to laugh at when recalling.

Managing To Please

"Early" pretty much said it all: early spring, early career, and Sunday morning, when early is all there can ever be.

The body-singer, never known for being the body-svelte, gave ample reason for what everywhere walked in circles, cupped its ears, twirled its arms, and made strange sounds: a host of bright eyes and bushy tails, revving up for a voice competition at the Turtle Bay Music School on Manhattan's Lower East Side. Full-figured or slim, east side or west, when you have to sing before noon, it is early.

The Baroque solo hymn my quite un-ample tail had started the competition with was a good waker-upper; in the last section, the word "Alleluia" repeats over and over, in this case serving to indicate whether the judges were paying attention. They were. As I sipped water and waited for their choice of a second selection, a sort of muted groan wafted up from that general direction: "Sounds like Mr. Purcell ran out of words."

The incipient wrinkles about my face scarcely camouflage faint smile, while behind them the instruments of sight were trying to locate the street person that had wandered in to say such a thing. Once the judges decided on the opera aria, I began to explain what I should have said in the beginning, namely that my pianist had not condescended to show up for the occasion and that a nice young…"Now, now, no excuses. No excuses." This time I could see it was the male judge blurting it out. "'Course, if he ran off with a girl, that's different!"

"Jesus!" I thought. "Who is this deviate?" A third wisecrack followed. Here I was in the all-too-short sleeves of my second-hand sport coat, trying to project a measure of dignity, against the background of some lowlife taking public pot shots at me.

Valiantly I apparently carried on. That evening a nice woman called to let me know that I had not only won the competition, but that one of the judges, a Mr. Lippman from a respected New York artist management, wanted me to contact him. One thing led to another, and in a few weeks that same living wisecrack had added me to an impressive roster of professionally managed singers. What I couldn't in my wildest excursions have imagined was that he was the highly respected, last of the old time singer agents; someone, moreover, that I would come to love like a father.

Rather, old time *"managers,"* I should say.

Joseph A. Lippman didn't like to be called an agent. The difference didn't just denote a lifetime of experience and different professional level. A manager took singers under his wing; he went with them to auditions, sheltered, cajoled, mentored and otherwise fought for them. Nor did he just collect the fee offers, or encourage you to take parts that weren't right for your voice for a quick agency buck. A manager made the business decisions on your behalf, you the artistic ones. Moreover, charging singers monthly retainers instead of mere commissions had been run out of the territory by his level of know-how, and by basic pride as well.

Manager Joe Lippman was even known to interrupt an audition in the middle: if the listeners weren't going to pay attention, he was taking his singer off the stage. An agent sets up the auditions; a manager sees you through them. Joe knew how to do all of that all right, but had garnered enough respect to sometimes book singers on his word alone. He said it was because he had never sold a dud.

Not that by any stretch was Joseph A. Lippman without his faults. The way I described him most often was that you adored him if he was on your side, couldn't stand him if he wasn't. He was the kind of person—better still, *personality*—you wanted in your corner fighting for your career. Though to be sure, it was a different age; then, he was mostly thought of as "a character;" in today's PC world, his approach just wouldn't fly- not that, knowing him, would he have altered it.

Nor was Joe one to forgive. He was not in the least kind to people who didn't repay his loyalty. On a more global sense, he seemed to hold every single German-born citizen- young or old- personally responsible for what the NAZIS had done to his people. As a rule, he didn't much care for coaches, conductors, or even musical repertoire from that part of the world. Nor would he handle a German artist, no matter how nice the manners, how beautiful the singing, or, I might add, how big a career the singer brought to the managerial table. Rumor had it that Joe had once bought a Carnegie Hall orchestra section ticket to a Dietrich Fischer-Diskau concert, just to get up and walk out as the singer came onto the stage. I never asked him if it was true, but wouldn't have put it past him.

One day Joe and I jumped in a cab, after having had lunched together. He gruffly told the driver where he wanted to go and precisely how, then added "AND TURN THAT THING DOWN!" The radio was playing and Joe wanted to talk. Turning around with his arm on the back of the front seat, the driver questioned Joe's tone. Joe responded with "I SAID," and repeated the whole thing, only louder, ending with "And I don't like people from other countries telling me what to do." We're not impressed with that kind of thing anymore.

In his office, Joe's assistant once told him that a young impresario was on the line and wanted to talk to him. Joe clearly *didn't* want to talk to *him,* but finally grabbed the phone: "Whatta you want, Driver- you don't have any money- you don't want 'ny good singers," took the place of "Hi, Bob. What could I do for you?" Not exactly the way it's done in today's anything-for-a-booking business.

Then again, Joe could be an absolute lamb. I remember his rising from his seat and walking around the back of the auditorium as I auditioned, giving me the "A-Okay" sign with his thumb and forefinger. He was a devoted family man, absolutely adored his daughter, and was incredibly proud that she was "decent." When she and her fiancé came to stay, Joe told the boy that he had her bedroom wired with electrical alarms and flashing lights. One touch from his hand on her doorknob would mean nocturnal bedlam.

And he loved children. He once doted on *my* daughter over lunch in a Chinese restaurant. For two hours I think he didn't stop joking with her. She loved it, but did bring him up short when he posed, "Now tell me Sarah; how is it a brown cow eats green grass and makes white milk?" Without hesitating, the three-year-old Center City Philadelphian replied, "They eat milkweed." It was the only time I ever saw Joseph A. Lippman at a loss for words.

Speaking of jokes, Joe had at least one for every occasion. When he signed restaurant checks, he'd say, "I'm writing this in disappearing ink, you know." If his stories were off color, then only mildly so, and I think he began every client phone call with one. But he himself was usually the best story.

Joe had invited me to his apartment one night when his wife was to be out. We were talking strategy, co-mingling it with playing records and relating his experiences with the great old time singers. Because his wife wasn't home, Joe was smoking a cigar. Suddenly, as if trying to catch him in the act, she bolted back through the front door like an elephant. Joe jumped up, shoved the slimy thing into my hand, and said, "Here, you smoke it." I laughed about that incident for days: a manager and his new 29-year old bass-baritone sat in his living room planning the kid's musically respiratory future while the boy puffed on a big smoke. I guess she bought it; I never heard otherwise.

By the time I met him, Joe Lippman was already becoming a little forgetful. He took notes of things you said, remarking that he never made a point to remember anything he wrote down. If he repeated the same story, I simply knew it meant he was telling the truth. Three times he told me that if he had had a son, he would have wanted him to be like me, each time adding, "I've only said that to two other people."

It was the kind of thing you took to the bank, but more than that, treasured. Joe would reminisce about the people he had managed. When he said something it was, by God, pitted against that backdrop and you'd better believe it. He would describe audience women's reaction to Ezio Pinza's bicyclist legs (not a dry seat in the house), or what Richard Tucker said ("What's that?") when he booked his first Verdi *Requiem*, or something else that Robert Merrill had done when he "started his career."

Joe Lippman managed to please, both himself and a lot of other people, and was born to do that very thing if ever anyone was. Though personal friends with the great performers of the '40s, '50s and '60s, he said it meant the more to him to do something for a neophyte like me, and that that something would never be a small role or one for a small fee! You went out of his office feeling like a million bucks because Joe said you were "going to have a big career, kid" and go in the Met "through the front door." More than once I made up a reason to stop by his office just because I knew it would pick me up.

But even Joe was mortal.

Toward the late '70s, he seemed to be ailing. Rumors were flying, agents turning cartwheels to attract his singers. Some were successful. One pretty big-name Italian tenor, whose career Joe had built from scratch in this country, left him.

Not that long afterward, the two ran into each other in the lobby of the New York State Theater. Totally guileless when face to face with Joe's preternatural weight loss, the tenor exclaimed, "Are you Meester Leepman?" Joe's response was typical and typically unflappable:

without missing a beat, he replied, "Yes. That's who *I* am. But I don't recognize *you*," and walked on.

Not long afterward, Joe collapsed while dining at a restaurant. Even in the hospital halls I *heard* him before I saw him, ordering the nurses and doctors around like crazy. While I sat by his bed, he played me tapes of his other singers. Then suddenly he looked up and asked me to turn something over for him. I didn't understand what, but eagerly rose and started to reach. "No, this," he said, pointing to himself. He couldn't roll over in bed, but had that acid humor.

In a few minutes I left so that he could take a chemo treatment; we agreed to see each other again in two days. But for once, the last of the old time managers didn't keep his word, or an appointment. The final treatment proved to be too much for him.

A lot of well-known opera singers showed up at his funeral. Amazingly, some of them even managed to sing one last time for the last of the old time managers. Others wept unabashedly throughout. If there was a dry eye in the entire synagogue before, then not a single one stayed that way after his doctor told us what Joe had demanded of him: he couldn't let him die because his "kids" needed him.

We did. And the world—most definitely the *singing* world—has never been the same since

On My Watch

The Missouri Bible Boy was off base, maybe blown off course, not so much by the wind in his sails as the draught in his swelled head. He had a wife and child back home, and a Scandinavian girlfriend in Vienna. Yet, here he was alone, walking the streets of Geneva, Switzerland for an entire month. It was competition time again, this one in the big arena.

Both heady and scary is how it all struck the "MBB,* he who until his upper class collegiate years had not so much as ventured beyond the "Show Me State" borders. The "MBB?" Well, that would be me.

Only baptism this time around wouldn't be by water, but by sheer fire. Poor and lonely, I also knew little French. I'd order *Ris di Veau* in a restaurant expecting veal, only to have a bowl of boiled pancreas plopped in front of me, accompanied by a smirk from the

*Abbreviation for Missouri Bible Boy

waiter. Neither hat nor coat being among my belongings, I caught cold in the central European fall air, mere days before singing my songs. I was nervous, and I was vexed.

And I felt otherwise stymied. The room they assigned me for Geneva Conservatory was the same space where the great Romanian performing artist, Dinu Lipatti, had taught piano. His pictures hung everywhere and haunted me, especially since I knew what he had accomplished in his short life, and just how short that was.

Of course, it was a miracle I had even heard of Lipatti. Thanks to the extracurricular education of Janet's family—largely by virtue of being invited to dinner—one of the musical figures I had learned of was Lipatti. We listened to recordings, read jacket blurbs, and wiped tears from our eyes at the account of his last recital when he was too weak to play the fourteenth Chopin waltz. Twenty years later—already an era of shortcuts and artistic fusion—I would use his example getting through to my own students: the pianist had once balked at committing to a

**My first wife

performance of the Beethoven *Emperor Concerto* because he wouldn't have a full five years to prepare it!

Still, it was not to take a full five days to realize how my introduction to Geneva was going. One of the competition adjudicators—who, having heard me the previous spring in Paris—saw me in the hallway and mentioned that I had been impressive in the opening round, though, putting his hand to his eyes to profess impartiality, added, "I don't see you." Ironically, he hadn't. The audition had taken place behind a screen, and he had only heard me.

The laying of contestant eyes on one another was something of a different story. There was only one other singer in the competition that I knew. Running into each other just before the first round of singing, we had trouble disguising the irrational competitive fear with which singers are normally smitten, though aspiring to make a mark in the ranks of a supposedly collaborative art form.

My intimidation was at least justified. This guy had won every other major singing competition in the western hemisphere, plus a couple in some other part of the world. I was six feet, two inches tall, he bigger still. But his paranoia inexplicably went to work on him, as mine, just as inexplicably, dissipated. Suddenly he seemed shorter and, for once, I realized I wasn't losing to myself, not this time, not on *my* watch.

Further underscoring the point, a somewhat elderly woman from the competition office, one Aline Baud-Bovy, took to me. Madame Baud-Bovy had no say whatsoever in the competition's outcome, but the word was apparently out and her befriending me told me I was the frontrunner. When she learned I was interested in wines, she invited me to a luncheon on her veranda, where we snacked and polished off an outstanding *Châteauneuf-du-Pape,* 1954, which, moreover, she had bottled herself. I listened to stories and looked at pictures, all of which were intoxicating by themselves, let alone with a *meritage* to the fine Rhône *vin rouge* we sipped.

Interestingly, Aline Baud-Bovy had helped sponsor Dinu Lipatti's first two public concerts. One had been in a downtown Geneva hotel lobby, where the young artist, though content with his playing, deduced from the mirrors looking back at him as he glanced from the keyboard, that he was ugly. Ugly he wasn't, and Madame Baud-Bovy rushed in with a Disney World of matronly and "patronly" reassurance.

It helped. Tickets to both performances had literally been given away. When the young pianist played again a short time later, the concert sold out in a day.

Back at the Geneva International Competition, it was time for all contestants who had made it to the final round to rehearse their opera aria with the conductor.

In all honesty, the guy was a decent sort, quiet-spoken, face heavily lined. When I got to know him better a few months later, I realized why. He had a wife in Switzerland and a girlfriend in Vienna, where he traveled every week to conduct at the *Volksoper*. I remember wondering if leading such a life would soon carve similar features upon my own countenance. I had a head start from the eyebrows up already.

When we met, I could see between his lines that my having shown up dressed in jeans and displaying an affable manner told him I was just another "Texan" who would never do justice to *King Phillip's Aria* from Verdi's **Don Carlo.** As an American, I would witness such reactions over and again. Of course, several of my school chums had gone before me in German-speaking operatic Europe, often doing little to assuage the impression. As was my bent, I "would" to assuage.

Kaiser- the conductor- stood at the piano with his nose in the score, never once looking up as long as I sang. But when I finished the last *"Amor' per me non ha,"* he slowly lifted his eyes and held my glance, the *scoring* on his face somehow seeming less pronounced.

We took the aria on tour after the competition, performing it in several old churches along the French border. The piece, with its majestic solo cello introduction, couldn't have been presented in more enhancing acoustics. A few weeks later, sitting in a Viennese café, Kaiser earnestly looked from the face of his girlfriend into that of my girlfriend, declaring that we never performed the aria together that it didn't move him. I think he meant it. After all, one can't lie in front of his mistress.

A decade thence, I would be gripped by one of my more famous True Nature searches, this time in the annals of what is now called classic (American) Country Music. In its infinite wisdom, the industry had produced a song called, "Trying to Love Two Women is Like a Ball and Chain." Every time that song came on the radio, I thought of Kaiser and wondered if he and his furrowed brow had finally succumbed, either to a fifty percent decrease in women, or to death itself.

On the competition's final night I was on top of the world, as the awards were passed out, nearly in orbit. I not only took first place, but kept getting called back to the stage for extra prizes. Revenge for my birthplace was especially sweet for one of them: someone had endowed a special accolade in the event first place went to an American. Additionally, there was an extra thousand francs for any contestant who won *a l'unanimité*, by a unanimous vote of the jury.

I did so win the competition (unanimously), plus, as it turned out, was the first male singer ever to do so: not such greats as Walther Berry or José van Dam, who had gone before, but me. I was incredulous when Madame Baud-Bovy pulled that little gem from the archives of her considerable mind.

Still, the most memorable gift I came away with was a beautiful gold Rolex timepiece, presented to me as a final recognition. On the back it read, *"Concours International d'Exécution de Musique de Gèneve Gary Kendall 1er prix, 1974."*

And so it went.

The Swiss Franc was high and life was good. The Rolex-tracked sun continued 'round the heavens, as I—sometimes—plodded along with it, not living up to the prognostications born of a magical fall month in a distant land to a mid-western kid with a broken compass.

But the experience remains a treasure, a frozen place in time that no one can ever take away. I have the proof. It's all right there, not so much etched into my comparatively smooth forehead, as upon yet another facade: it is On My Watch.

A Swallowty of Life Thing

We called him "Kalle Sju" for short and teased him that the sobriquet sounded something like "call a shoe." The joke was hardly lost on him, his English being perfect, and humor being something he most definitely sensed. But some forty years later, neither is a sort of irony lost on me—since at the time he was almost as old as I am now—that what I really called ol' Kalle was, "my friend."

Karl Sjunnesson, alias Kalle Sju, lived just outside Stockholm in Bromma—and apparently always alone, which must have accounted for a tendency to lecture: "If you can't take time to sit down to a meal, I-mean-what-the-hell, you're-too-busy!" Easy for him; gourmets always eat lavishly.

But in truth, it wasn't so easy. An arts freelancer in a tax-torn country, Kalle Sju was usually broke. Still he ate well, like a king in fact, and normally made quite the production of it.

In his day, Kalle had landed an—unexpectedly *en Français*—interview with American composer Samuel Barber in Paris, and in Rome sold a used car to a future pope. He wrote for newspapers, compiled cookbooks, authored and produced a ton of TV shows. Even his most frequent dinner guests were *strictly* forbidden to wash dishes, while every room of his house displayed the same wallpaper: floor-to-ceiling books.

What came to be known as his "stories"—mostly personal experiences—dragged on and on, yet rarely failed to amuse. My favorite detailed the sailing of his converted 1949 Norwegian fishing boat all the way to the south of France. Only Kalle Sju, *of course*, did it his own way: keeping to a self-designed "AAA Triptych" of rivers and inland canals, not a single wave of saltwater lapped up the sides of that old trawler once he exited the Baltic.

> But with all the food and all the fun,
> I never knew Kalle to eat on the run.

Sometimes he'd call up to borrow money. At others, those startling blasts from the wall ringer were like the Nordic "Ma Bell" summoning you: Kalle'd been paid for some project and the festivities were commencing. And, my, how we did feast then! If I timidly were to suggest saving his money for a rainier day, he'd just grumble something about blowing it all right away being the only way to prove he was a true freelancer. When the coffers ran low, we'd manage a final sauté and flûte of champagne waiting for the cab back to Stockholm, as I recall arranged and prepaid by the man himself.

> But don't you think, and wouldn't you know?
> I never saw Kalle eating on the go.

Home to me in those days was the apartment of my Swedish squeeze, in the heart of that most beautiful of northern European cities. Not that I can say I much got along with the rest of the family. When Mommy Dearest came in from the country, the baggage she brought was fear of audibly passing gas. The WC in that particular *Pied-à-Terre* was a tad too close to where we slept and I had to move out for a few days. Incensed at this rudeness, Kalle Sju would come to my rescue.

On one such occasion, the true freelancer gods had truly smiled. At around 1:00 in the afternoon, he- did I say the former car salesman didn't drive?- swung by in a Mercedes taxi and whisked me off for lunch at the Opera Cellar; it was the finest restaurant in all of Scandinavia. After a small repast of "lax pudding," Aquavit chased with beer, dessert and a tour of the complete restaurant (remodeled and managed by a friend of his), we hailed yet another Benz bound for Bromma.

Nej-hej," but the culinary entertainment wasn't over. About halfway there, Kalle Sju instructed the driver to pull up in front of a grocery, where the driver and I, *and* the running meter, waited for Kalle to lay in a goodly store of victuals. I was his guest, you see; helping was *naturally* not allowed. Arriving home, he set about making a wonderful dinner that culminated with yet another dessert, Italian coffee, French cognac and one of Fidel's personal favorites, proffered every single time from the original box, and accompanied by the same melodious, "Cigar?"

It was simply the way the man lived. If his *Små Franska* pastry, espresso, Monte Cristo and scratch pad were the morning ritual, then— what-the-hell!—even his diet menus would have to oblige with the obligatory bubbly in the evening. But never, though constantly busy with a million projects:

> The devil take me should I lie,
> Was Kalle tempted by treats on the fly.

Now, my old friend wouldn't have approved of what I saw the other day while crossing Broadway. A young woman sat behind the wheel of a minivan as she prepared to turn right onto 79th Street. Waiting for the light, she availed herself of the opportunity to stuff the better part of a stuffed pastry into her mouth. The fishtail motion of the vehicle, once it began to inch through the crowd, told me her hands were just a "scone" too full to drive. Alas, the gentleman next to her wasn't of much use; earphones firmly embedded, he held savory treats of his own, and resided somewhere on the outskirts "la-la" land.

An overt tragedy connected to this little story there isn't, though a dash of *Weltschmertz* for anyone inclined to cast even a slapdash glance at contemporary life. Everyone knows what Shakespeare called the whole world. Today, I half wonder if he would have said "restaurant." You know:

> Food is not food, which alters where alteration of snack bar
> Finds, nor bends with the waste remover to remove.

> Oh, no! 'Tis an ever-fixed choke,
> The constant gag of every wandering bloke!

Not a day goes by that I don't see people munching in a dozen different venues not designed for the act, including filth-layered New York subway cars. You expect Central Park carriage horses to chomp their oats from the street. But I'm a little taken aback to see the drivers nibbling alongside, mere inches from a recently executed poop-shoot.

I've even known my students to bring food to their voice lessons. Strongly counseling them not to consume and tune at the same time, I still find paper cups and napkins about the studio, and on the antique cherry table outside our front door.

*

Experienced and wise, Kalle Sju influenced me enormously and I miss him. Sad but true is that I've lost touch; I don't know where he is or that he's even alive. If able to wiggle still, he's dodging the tax authorities and not answering his phone anyway.

Plus, the last time I tried I got sidetracked. Waiting for the international connection, a dollop of my egg-and-olive sandwich dripped onto the open laptop. In my haste to get both phone and sandwich into one hand so as to brush off the keys with the other, I bashed the back of *it* into a Styrofoam Cup, spilling coffee onto the printer. Those events then commanding my lips to utter a forceful fricative imprecation, I sprayed a pasty, pre-digested combo of solid food and libation into the mouthpiece, forgot all about the call to Sweden and hung up the phone, gluing it to the base ringer.

But I loved 'ol Kalla Sju,
Who never dined, had he one thing left to do.

Thimik, Not Mimic

Mastery of a foreign language is a twofold affair: on one hand there is the linguistic structure, on the other, indigenous sounds. Despite software shortcuts, the structure part is universally thought to be a mental chore, whereas mastering the sounds is essentially a question of refined mimicry. The older a person is, the more separated the two parts normally become, and the more difficult it is to gain proficiency.

We adults, moreover, battle ourselves. Small children, renowned for their grasp of speech elements, accomplish the feat by an undisturbed synthesis of the above tenets. They do not plague themselves with the defense mechanisms and perfectionist pleasures with which grownups stumble through life. But we forget that those same children are not only fed initial heaps of help with the language, but spend most of the rest of their academic lives studying that same subject, despite having darkened the first grade door doing just fine with it.

The *Suzuki* method of teaching musical instruments is based on a similar premise. Mr. Suzuki, a musician and wounded World War II soldier, is said to have lain in his hospital bed, observing that the swarms of refugees about his ward learned to speak the Japanese language just as quickly as any other children, despite being homeless, sick, and half starved. The filmed results of his subsequent experiments, featuring tiny tots playing quarter-sized violins with amazing virtuosity, are legendary. Those children often did not read a note of music. Refined mimicry indeed!

As an adult foreign language grammar student, I was not all that hot. I can get around in two or three of them today and did teach myself Swedish well enough to sing in it and be interviewed over National Swedish Television. The interviewer, one Karl Sjunnesson, did go on and on about how I had picked it up. No slouch linguist himself, he duly complimented me.

In most cases, though, I was beset by the same tendency I have in English: I am **too literal** and often miss the linguistic forest for the syntactical trees. I may be so preoccupied at not perfectly understanding some nuance–the first few words of a sentence perhaps, or how someone phrases something–that I fail to hear what follows. That tendency is especially critical in German, where the most important word is frequently the last one of the sentence!

I am, *however*, something of a mimic. If you utter some human, or other, noise, the chances are good that I can do it back to you, and make you laugh in the process. This dubious talent, exercised alongside my "singerly" tendencies, has enabled me to navigate in a handful of spheres, won me a few free beers, and, yes, landed me in some hot water. More pejoratively, the penchant places me in positions whereby, sounding better that I in fact am, people speak back to me unintelligibly quickly.

Along similar lines, I quite naturally talk for animals, uttering things in a voice that might reflect what they would say and sound like, if able to talk. People have been known to find this curious habit funny as well, especially when involving mutated animal "cuss" words. A few others, I might add, have also found it tasteless.

One language that fascinates me is Chinese. I adore the Chinese people and, also their food. I don't speak that language, but was once taught to say a few things by an airline hostess friend. Those phrases have gotten me extra dumplings in restaurants and puffed me up with male pride on a number of real swell occasions.

In my college days, I was somewhat known for doing the referred-to impressions, that even provided me with a professional experience or two in connection; in other words, I got paid. And, okay, I admit that one of my favorites was that of a stereotypical, exaggerated Asian, accent. *Never* did any of this have thing one to do with ridiculing anyone, but rather signaled a life-long propensity to do almost anything for a laugh, or a buck.

Any fool, however, knows that what goes around comes around. Sometimes, because I have both goofed off so much and/or been so **literal** trying to figure out what someone meant, I am often not taken seriously when not joking at all, nor just when doing it onstage.

Zum Beispiel, as the Germans say (for example), in the late 1970s, my young daughter and I were traveling in Europe. At a train stop in Northern Italy, a couple of students from Taiwan boarded the train and sat in our compartment. These students were adorably pleasant and spoke *our* language quite well. After a few minutes, my daughter embarrassed me by suddenly, and rather loudly, yanking on my sleeve, blurting out, "Daddy, do your Chinese imitation for them!!"

Later, however, when I tried to smooth the whole thing over by asking one of them how to say something in Chinese, I repeated it by abandoning myself, quite subconsciously, to the method I always did doing my party imitations. When I did, the two students looked at each other in astonishment, then back at me, and replied, "I-should-nev-er have-ex-pected-to-hear-it-said-so-well-by-a-for-eig-ner!"

The *coup de grâce,* or I should say the *coup de marriage,* of my linguistic comeuppance, nevertheless occurred while living in Cincinnati, specifically on an evening when I was searching for a Chinese restaurant. Kathy and I had joined one of those dining clubs; you know the type: buy a meal and get the second free. After about a month of Kathy's innate frugality and my insatiable singer's appetite, we had exhausted the booklet's offerings, that is, except for one obscure "Hunan" place. Not knowing the location, I called to get directions, while my better half half-listened from the next room reading a magazine.

The place in question was an authentic Chinese restaurant; in other words, most of the people in charge, as well as the customers, were themselves native Chinese, including the woman who answered the phone. When she told me the streets that formed the intersection where the restaurant was located, I repeated them aloud just as she had said them: "**SHEE-MO, LID-DING,**" she and I both said, followed by my mumbling something to the effect of not quite believing I knew where that particular junction was.

I am not exaggerating, now. A second time I asked the name of the streets and repeated it, clueless as to what she meant, though having been on those streets dozens of times.

Better said, with frighteningly little *refinement* attached to this mimicry, I was falling back on my tendency to simply repeat what I heard without putting any part of my brain in gear. "No," she insisted a second time. "Shee-mo Lid-ding," sounding to me not only as she had uttered it the first time, but as I had said it back to her, so that we were getting nowhere, and fast. "Shee-moo Lid-ding" we again went into over and over like an operatic duet, on my part merely uttering it aloud as one will do wondering about something.

Kathy, it is important to know, was already working as a minister; a minister I say, in one of the local churches, and, in addition, always had this way of walking quite unministerially, with large arm swing from the elbow upward, especially when in a hurry, or otherwise agitated.

Suddenly, about that time, she therefore bolts into the room like a cross between a pregnant water buffalo and Don Quixote tackling yet a second windmill, and in this sort of growl-whisper, seethes, "Seymour and Reading, *goddammit!* They'll think you're making fun of them!!"

With apologies to both the Chinese and the Cincinnati Ministerial Alliance, please Seymour Reading on the following pages.

Linville On Loan

"He was a real guy" is the way I learned to say it in Kentucky-Speak. It wasn't so much that I didn't hear the phrase elsewhere, applied to other folk; just that this real guy fit the appellation real well.

I met real guy Houston Linville in the middle of a hayfield on a hot July day in 1986, asking if he would bale what little hay I had in my front field "for half." He didn't say, "Hello," not, "Nice to meet you," nothing. He just listened, nodding his head, almost imperceptibly, from his tractor seat. It was the kind of nod that nevertheless rocks the upper torso slightly and instills trust. Immediately, I thought Houston Linville a real nice guy.

Over the next fifteen years or so, Houston did bale my hay. And he plowed my garden and he spread my topsoil and he tore down my old garage just for the materials. And he kept an eye on my place when I was away, let me take diesel from his barrel, electric from his barn. He apologized for tearing up my fence and, unlike others, refrained from making fun of me when I flailed and floundered, surviving in the country.

And he told me when he was tired of looking at an old stump in my pasture, pushed it out with his new tractor, made sure I knew to put *my* tractor in the right gear before starting downhill, and to turn *up*hill when "bush-hogging." He came over with my dog when she was run over chasing another tractor the way his dogs had taught her, let me ride my horses on his land, cut firewood from his woods, and haul rock from his creek bed. He was a real neighbor.

Shortly after I moved to rural Kentucky, people started piping up with all sorts of free advice. At the top of the list was that I should never get a front-end loading tractor, 'cause everybody'd want to borrow it. Well, I gave new meaning to that counsel. My carpenter and I used Houston's "front-ending" John Deere for everything under the non-Tuscan sun.

Once while hoisting an 8x8x12 green oak lintel for my new barn, the thing rocked backward a quarter of a turn with a loud "BAM!" that threatened to crush Houston where he sat on the tractor seat. Screaming wildly, I jumped up and chained the thing to the bucket, but Houston acted like he hardly noticed. I thought him a real brave guy.

Sometime later, Houston junked that tractor and I couldn't help wonder if I had caused it. But Houston never said anything. Nor did he seem to mind when I apologized for my dog's running over to his house all the time, or chasing behind him as he walked between the house and barn. He just paused; then with that same head motion, muttered, "Kinda enjoy 'er." If we met on the road or in town, his greeting was similar to when I met him, only more- a sort of half bow. I thought Houston a real friend.

Houston Linville always helped me so much I was glad when I could return the favor: "Got one in mind," he responded one day, typically omitting the sentence subject. That favor was to listen to his musically inclined son to see if he really was any good, or at least advise him. On another occasion he said he'd borrow my horse trailer to haul his calves in.

Linguistics being part of my real business, I paid attention to the way he said certain words, like "calves," ("caves"), 'cause I didn't want to sound like some derned city hillbilly. But I noticed he drew the line at saying, "seal" for "sill," "chimley" for "chimney," "piss elm" for "elm," worser" for "worse" or "fetus" for "feces," like some other people out there did, and I thought Houston a real smart guy.

Along the road we lived on, which the one-man judge, jury and executioner of the county highway department deemed unworthy of a shoulder or center stripe, meeting another vehicle could be a thrill-a-minute.

Then too, it taught you a lot about your neighbors. On a progressive good-ol'-boy scale, hand waving said it all. The other guy's heading for the ditch at the last second, not slowing down a lick and trying to fake you out got the lowest rating. Lifting an index finger atop the steering wheel while maintaining his speed or slowing down only slightly, took second place from the bottom.

The free hand, raised normally, is a good indicator of a man's character on any terrain. That same hand, though, stuck straight in the air, rotating like a weather vane spoke volumes, whereas waving broadly afterward demonstrated the best a native Kentucky son was capable of.

Billy Evans, who lived a mile or so down the same byway, was one of the nicest guys I ever met. Billy was the weather vane type of country road combatant, slowing down drastically ahead of time, pulling over, sometimes even stopping to let you pass, while half-turning his vertically raised hand to wave.

But Houston, our Houston Linville, following a similar genetic impulse, pulled quite into the ditch, stopped stock-still and bowed, bowed I say, from his truck seat. No roadway on earth was ever traversed by a more real human being.

Houston said his reason for working a second full time job on that farm of his was that he liked watching things grow. I think he did. I guess it was why he had to finish cultivating his tobacco one afternoon before checking into Meadowview Hospital that evening for the heart attack he had that morning. We laughed about it in is his room, but, underneath, I thought Houston a real crazy guy.

Part of what he taught me over the years came through parable-like stories of his parents, and I got to where I could beat him to the punch quoting his father. Late in his mother's life, he moved her into a mobile home across the road from my hayfield. When Houston mowed, raked and baled my hay, he'd wave to his mother where she sat on that little front porch of hers every single time he came around, just like it was the first time he'd seen her that day. And he walked over to my house to tell me when she died, though he waited for me to ask how she was. I thought Houston a real son.

In that same mobile home, Houston Linville later housed tobacco workers from Mexico. Some of them became the permanent friends that he on more than one occasion drove home far south of the border after the King Burly housing season, and, at other times, visited.

Downtown at the Corner Café in Augusta, I lunched with a number of people over the years who had worked under Houston at the plastics factory he had managed, long since before I moved there. It is a world in which being permanently suspicious of—even hating—the boss is a way of life. If there was ever a negative thing said about boss Houston, though, I never heard it, even from a couple he had fired. It was obvious they thought Houston a real fair guy.

The foregoing is the reason Houston amazed me one afternoon, even more than usual. Some guy up the road had apparently done something really bad. Houston wouldn't even tell me what it was. Said Houston only, "I was so mad right then that if I'd seen him, I'd uh... ... I'd uh killed him," nodding his head a little more than ordinary. Coming from a guy I never even saw show annoyance, that statement kind of rocked me back on my heels, and made me realize that said act was a bad one indeed. For once I thought Houston a real scary guy.

A stonemason friend and I were finishing building my outdoor grill one day and remarked it was big enough to roast a pig in. Observing the project's final stages and that remark, Houston said, well, he'd furnish the pig, and went over and shot it. We ate off that damned thing for days, and I thought Houston a real generous guy.

It wasn't long before Houston Linville died that I learned he thought a lot of me. People don't much talk about things like that in rural Kentucky. Apparently his feelings were mostly based on the way I worked, kind of non-stop, on my property, and that I wasn't a snob.

Darned if I didn't always mean to tell him I liked him too. I thought I had lots of time. And then I forgot to let him know his spud bar he said he never liked to use anyway, was in my barn all the years since I built it. And I sure intended to apologize to him after Kathy's parents kind of snubbed him, being from Kentucky and all, especially since he and his wife had been nice enough to come over just to say "hello." But Houston never said anything. In fact, I thought him a real polite guy.

You know, every time I hear that Larry Gatlin song, "Houston Means That I'm One Day Closer To You," I think of him; always did and for sure always will. It's even spelled the same.

So Houston, if you're paying attention, I really did always like you a lot, even though we hardly ever talked, especially in the last years when I was back and forth to New York. I thought I was lucky to have you as a neighbor when so many people have bad ones. Like that same song says, we *are* a day closer to you. You're only on loan from us anyway, and you know what else? Seeing you will be the best part about being on the other side, cause you are, *still*, a *REAL* GUY!

Institutions of Lower Learning

"They don't learn anything," she more tossed off than enunciated, she who constantly deals with the commodity, she who in me had a willing ear, she who was dead on the money, and she who was Arlene.

The abject shame of it all was not just that she was right, or even had reason to utter it. It was the attitude; the—to her—quite un-native resignation, when to almost anyone, professional or amateur, it should elicit gasps. Be that as it may, you can etch it in stone: voice majors graduate from Bachelors programs, sometimes with Master Degrees, anywhere in this country ignorant as light poles.

And why wouldn't they? Today, a music school is just another business. Many if not most music majors never go into music. Administrators, one of two main branches of musical performance washouts (newspaper critics being the other: "Critics are like eunuchs; they try but can't.") seldom trouble themselves with quality. They don't mind it, understand, just worship at the altar of numbers. Well, numbers and their standing in the thirty-four professional associations they belong to. Numbers get funds, and it is not uncommon to receive a mild higher-up hand slap, signifying your faculty-based desire for admissions refinement. These musical assembly-lines produce people who not only don't have an inkling of what it means to be professional, but what the profession of (in my field, for instance) voice performance even is, including specialty-related areas they are interested in enough to major. "Here is your degree, now go get your education" was never so appropriately advised as to a voice graduate. The goal up to this point has, after all, been getting by.

But then, classrooms are poor places to learn anyway. Adamant as I once was in favor of formal education, I don't know if I would even matriculate had I to do it over, and would be absolutely degreeless if aiming for a performing career. In schools you learn by belching up for a grade that which someone else said. Only, you can't do anything you don't own; can't truly own anything you can't learn to do, can't truly learn anything you didn't experience. Oh well, most of their teachers couldn't either (which is why they teach), providing one with spurious sources of mentoring *von Anfang an.* *

* German for "From the beginning."

When I was a student at Indiana University—known already as a factory in the music business in the1960s—faculty and student recitals alike drew hordes that arrived early for a seat; the rest hung from the balconies, sometimes precariously just to gain the experience. Nor was it because they took place in an obscure, mid-western town where there was little else to do. Today you can't buy a school audience. You put your academic *derrière* on the line presenting a challenging faculty program for the students of your own performing area whom you naively think care anyway, only to discover a large portion of them in the lounge doing their music theory assignments as you are on your way to the stage for the performance. I had "anti-faculty viruses" too, way back when. Unlike the resistant mutations of today, though, I attended anyway, knowing I could always learn from the experience.

~~~

My own pathway to the swivel chair desk of academia accompanied the full flowering of "The Age of Entitlement and Victimization," ushered in by a way of approaching art that I myself never dreamed of, unless truly, *truly* I say, I was mistreated.

Where I first taught, most students, lucky to be on full scholarship, seldom imbibed the cool draught of responsibility. Searching the minds of other teachers in other schools, with or without the academic free ride, I would get the same response: student apathy and arrogance, or was it *ignorance* and arrogance, either a curious tandem resident of the same cranium.

To my students, I was seldom a living being so much as a device, something plugged in to serve what *they thought* were their needs. True, I was paid for it and, you say, surely not so bad that they should have seen me that way. The irony existed in the curious reversal of roles: if they knew so much, why would they be in school anyway?

Throw in the ring the hat of today's students being given a large, tail-wagging say in who is hired (or retained) as faculty, through the process of evaluations, and, believe it or not, positions on search committees! And the beat goes on.

Or, rather, doesn't.

The single most astounding issue specific to voice teaching is singers' musicianship. How many other curricula are populated with those who have little background in the majoring subject, are cavalier about it moreover, and proceed through the various levels happily propped upright and taking free nourishment? In singing, we think we have to pamper; worse still, the candidates expect it.

A musical instrumentalist before I was a vocalist, pampering was not part of the agenda. If you came in musically wrong in an ensemble, you were likely to get a subtle reminder, something hurled back at you like, "I'll give you a hint, Dipshit; what was Basie's first name?"

Most one-on-one sessions typical of voice instruction are not lessons at all, but handholding bolstering of a sort, spoon-feeding students in the learning of their music so that they can fulfill requirements. Having to "teach people notes," for all intents and purposes, indicates that they can't effectively read music. In precious few instances is a college voice teacher allowed to impart the finer details for which she trained, and, supposedly, hired. Too much time is taken up repeating the ABCs of music.

The first student that transferred out of my academic studio did so because I gave her a "B" when, in her mind, she was "better" than any of my other students. I pointed out that she had a more mature voice, which she should have going for a Bachelor's Degree at age thirty-two, but that in any other course what is required is learning the subject matter. That subject, in fact, didn't matter to her.

My second transferee did so because I had the gall to not support him in a proposed casting assignment in a fully staged school opera production. Frankly, I don't remember if I did or didn't. But, having the single tightest vocal production that to this day I have ever wrestled to improve, he had no business performing *any* role, much less the one in question. My reward for protecting his future, instead of his collegiate status, was his exit, saying to a friend, "If you can't depend on your own teacher to support you, well..." Today he is a college teacher himself, no doubt having owned, experienced, and otherwise learned that there is little quite so bad as witnessing a protégé self-destruct in public. More recently I learned that there was more to the whole move, including student-student and student-teacher sexually-based political practices.

Instead of examining themselves, most vocal student malcontents, leave their teachers in search of the next magic formula. Usually, they wind up with the same thing being said to them the former teacher did, thinking it now the word of God by way of a bolt of lightning.

Ask any teacher who ever sat through a master class in which his student performed. When the so-called "master" suggests something, the student does it right away. Yet it is very likely the same thing the "trench" instructor has stressed a dozen times with little result. When I give master classes, I take a moment to make clear that any progress I am apt to make has much more to do with the day-in-day-out, true instructor.

When singer-students do advance, it is predictable that they will scratch and claw for it themselves, beyond what they acquire in the classroom or vocal studio, making voice teaching a kind of guided "self-unfoldment," or supervised self-teaching. I recently saw a post on Face Book, saying something to the effect that the teacher can open the door, but the student has to go through it. If not so inclined, however, no amount of inspiring, cajoling, or letter grade threatening has a good chance of making much difference. They will blame anything negative on something or someone else, especially if the "someone" is willing to do what any true educator does: go the extra mile, often involving being honest to the point of saving the student from years of future regrouping. But rarely does such a good deed go unpunished.

Should it matter, then, that the graduating legions will tardily have to switch to another field to excel, that they will never gainfully be employed in music, or that they are mere tools of individual faculty, school size, and administrative advancement? After all, they now have a college degree.

The answer is that it matters a great deal, since it is *lives* of which we speak, each year of which is precious. A voice degree, plus two and half dollars, will get you a ride on any New York subway.

~~~

The genesis for many of the above problems still lies with admission policies of the school. Voice majors seldom are tested for music *or* language aptitude before entering college programs. Though supposedly qualified to navigate in the foreign "speaks" they routinely sing in, they manage to graduate linguistic idiots. If among a select few, they may be able to pronounce and translate the meagerest of poems in German, Italian and French. But don't "bet the ranch on it." In truth, I was the exception, which lead me to solving certain problems myself for which my teachers were not providing solutions. I can remember spending time in the university libraries, learning from great performing artists, that which I was not getting in my curricula. At times it led to giving certain instruction to my own teacher(s).

I am amazed at what today can pass for a (vocal/musical) coaching, and am always reminded of comedian Jeff Foxworthy's brilliant comic routine, "You Might Be A Redneck," in which he would go into a seemingly endless number of scenarios that would qualify one.

Vocal coaching (as opposed to a voice *lesson)* should include work in musical accuracy, interpretation, and language, as opposed to vocal technique. Quite tempting is to construct a Foxworthy-like routine based on singers' habits: if your idea of a coaching is to have the coach/pianist play through the notes of, or put on tape, pieces you are sworn to learn, you might be a dumb singer! But it is the world we live in.

Then again, students often follow the example tendered them by the faculty. Winston Churchill said something to the effect that the reason for the brutality of academia is that the stakes were so low. Faculties replace a former love for music with one of conspiracy. They bicker and politick behind colleagues' backs, connive for what a school should be according to the doctrine of self-promotion, all the while demonstrating nary a hint of recognition that disciples come and go, colleagues remain behind to continue wrestling over the problem that evolved with the student. They hesitate not to pit one part of an institution against another for private gain, gladly embodying, "Divided we stand, united we fall, and who gives a good goddamn."

Then there are the committee meetings, those bastions of lofty strategic out-mapping, seldom resulting in anything of import, tabling till next time being the common order of the day. Things that require evaluation are masses of convolution amounting to hills of beans that no

Jack could ever climb. In even five years, let alone a hundred, who would know the difference of what is "time-consumingly" charted and changed, or have the remotest part of an existence improved by it? The process is what I called being academically bound and gagged.

For one of my students' Master's oral exam at University of Cincinnati, the long-time music theory teacher appointed to the committee objected to the type of instruction the student had received by one of his own departmental colleagues. He asked a question about a Mozart symphony that the student didn't know, and said so. In the conference afterward, I said that it had not been fair because the student was not given a chance to show what he knew in other areas. The music *history* representative agreed with me and we overrode the music theorist. The student passed his orals without answering a single question about music theory. Worse still, I believe the theorist sought that very outcome, just to make a point.

For the vocal inadequacies that do surface, colleagues often use them as fodder for advancing their own reputations, frequently refusing to go with recommendations to demote or fail the students and whispering that it was, after all, the colleague's fault. Though not limited to this method, certain applied music (performance) professors get on a track of perceived brilliance, often from making their students feel cozy. After all, many roads lead to a vocal Rome and feeling comfortable is something of a helpful ingredient. But I saw very few conductors and stage directors who continued that practice in the post-graduate, real professional world.

Sometimes faculty intriguers get their political messages to prospective students through proselytizing networks. Those teachers are not without ability, especially that of making people *think* they are great teachers. They often are super-obese, earth-mama types, with a gift of gab and an otherwise acid tongue.

One such person joined the faculty on which I taught, and developed a big reputation in almost no time. Her favorite implement was taking students entrusted to her in summer apprentice programs and stealing them in the process. If the student—out of a sense of loyalty—balked at switching from the (usually wonderful) regular teacher, the sharp-tongued response was something like, "Jane, don't be a Pollyanna." It happened over and again, while the reputations of those teachers who were too ethical to do such a thing suffered.

~~~

I must nevertheless concede that all is not completely lost in true, usually state-supported academia. There, one has at least a procedure; a hierarchy for dealing with problems that an administrator can hide behind when he/she wants, also ignore if so motivated. The rules, though, do exist.

The "Big City" independent music schools go about it differently. They pay lip service to such insufferable documents as bylaws and mission statements, and a pretense for disciplinary structures to back them up. But there is no chain of command that, in and of itself, has "teeth." You can get fired with no recourse; also stay forever when you shouldn't, and for God only knows what category of reason.

In the New York City school where I was hired to impart vocal technique, instructors in allied areas were unabashedly giving free advice on that very subject (voice technique), in place of what they were hired to do. These areas should have included musical coaching, languages and acting, their instructors occasionally feeling the aforementioned administrative hand slap, only to resume what they were doing before the annoying little interruption.

There are at least three things wrong with said practice: the instructor is doubtfully qualified in the self-appointed area; the student does not get instruction her or she needs in the *allied* area, and it makes the job of his/her regular voice instructor twice as difficult, attempting to instill classical concepts in a sea of power politics. Still this well nigh ubiquitous practice goes on, often mixed with veiled (or not so veiled) professional pressure to students, often from someone recognized as a prominent figure in the field. That very power, even one of suggestion, is never so strong as to a group of would-be professionals (singers) who, at their best, can audibly sense (hear) almost nothing of what they actually sound like while in the act of phonating. In other words, the singing animal has some reason to be insecure about its art from note one. Enter yet another level of vulnerability.

I cannot count how many students at the above school told me that the big name vocal coaches (again, as opposed to actual vocal *teachers*) employed there found it virtually impossible to coach without bringing up the subject of sex, constantly drawing analogies through language and music, in most cases male on male.

Ah, but I lie. One female singer did say that one of them instructed her to shape her [o] vowel as if she were putting her mouth around a "great big African penis." Actually, I lie again. She was not a current student, merely the (previously-graduated) wife of one of the leading faculty administrators and teachers in the same field, one who, by the way, said he always admired the way I spoke my mind, at least until I resigned.

Early in my own student days, I had the confidence that, amidst the diminishing congregation of human decency, there were three remaining protective covers under which I could depend to not encounter subhuman behavior: churches, synagogues and colleges. Every place I went to school, every place I taught, and nearly every school I ever heard about, reeked of that very odor.

~~~

Clearly, a long time has passed since the aforementioned student days, so much so that few of my teachers are still at it, or even alive. The ones who are tell me what I thought I would never hear from them: that they have altered their approach, suppliant, just like the rest of the mainstream.

Of course, not everything was good about the old way either. In their heyday, the older teachers dictated everything, were known to throw things, gossip about the resistant ones, and otherwise dole out insults. One even brought me into her studio ahead of my lesson time just to show off for me, giving a directive, slamming the piano and shouting, "NOW GET IT!" to the student. Today we call such things teacher abuse and even have articles devoted to the subject in métier magazines. But being often led to believe that I have trouble detecting which is a tail and which is a dog, I won't expire from holding my breath waiting for the magazine series that treats the subject of "student" abuse.

~~~

Dog or tail, only time can tell how far it will go. But I do know this: with all that is available to current singing students for learning tools, there is infinitely less reason to been uninformed than ever. The trend is, however, in the opposite direction. Students were once concerned with getting the kind of training they needed. More recently, scholarship dollar and performance opportunity *within* the school determine where they attend.

And I notice that poverty, and being "busy" are the rationalizations for things they don't get accomplished, both as school students, and private (post-graduate) ones who don't come for lessons regularly. And I notice their cell phones, trendy clothes, cars, and funds for visiting lovers on other continents. Previously noted, I am "old fuck."

~~~

Dining with a professional singer I knew in New York already a few years back, an interesting revelation found its circuitous way to the light of conversation. The singer was going on about having had the misfortune of performing a work in which some college students were given the opportunity to do the smaller parts; it was what should have been a coveted and valuable experience for them. The professional singer I refer to was appalled at the level of preparation, attitude, and overall unprofessionalism the students displayed.

My reaction was that she was simply showing, not really her age, which wasn't at all advanced, but her lack of acquaintance with the current crop of vocal hopefuls. She simply did not believe me when I detailed my standard "teacherly" observations, complete with illustration, in particular that that which she had observed was the norm.

This woman earned at least one degree from the school of my first full time academic appointment, and not that long before I leapt into the ranks of assistant professors. Because of the standards she conformed to there, my impression was she thought me someone who had been eating a lot of sour grapes, a fuddy-duddy, or simply one who dreams these things up.

But I'll hang on. She is a truly nice person and will probably one day be sending me a mildly apologetic email. Many, if not most, singing professionals turn to voice teaching or coaching eventually. When and if she does so, she will get an earful from the "git-go".

In her save-the-world freshness, she may attempt to be the exception, showing my description doesn't have to be at all cynical. She may set some boundaries, "crack the whip" with her students. She may come through her attempts at hard-knock school issues that show up in bi-annual evaluations and reappointment files. Those evaluations, you may recall, would partly be filled out by those who came in hoping for an education, and now play a preternaturally decisive role in the professional life and death of those who were dealing with the commodity before the students were born.

But reading her email to me, my gin and tonic will taste extra good. I'll be, you see, vindicated; her first month on the job will have taken care of it.

Refrains From A K-9 *Chor*

As Half Read/Half Told By Judge Elroy "Booker" Beam, Bourbon County, Kentucky When My Leg was broke, and Using Two Witnesses Grabbed From The Courthouse Hallway, Who I Got Married By

Darned if Dad wasn't always thumbs-down on dawgs. 'Course the way the mangy things ran over town it 'as no 'onder. Even so, his quip 'bout forty years later to Kathy," 'Ull-you can't have a farm without a dawg!" rocked both of us back on our heels.

But they were free rangin' all right back 'kin, at least in small towns. I guess what that means is if you could 'a' ate one, it'd'a been better for you, and tasted better too. And a dime'd sure got you 'bout a dozen of 'em. Still, tears never ran down these cheeks more than when that ol' stray I'd claimed for my own died on the vet's table. Dad dropped t'at little bomb on me in front of the dry goods store after school and barely slowed down to do it.

After her came the bobtail I took to be put down myself. My dad tried to act like he didn't like that dog neither, but more than once I found the grouchy ol' thing (the dawg, I mean) in the back o' his print shop. I never could figure out, if underneath, the cantankerous old thing (Dad, that is) just liked the company or didn't want him takin' a hunk outta his customers like he (the dog, this time) had the Nyberg kids. Wiley thing (the dawg), he'd hang back about a block following Dad to town and then plop down right in front of the front door. Even running two businesses, God knows my dad had precious few customers the way it was.

Then, I think, came that arthritic birddog I sold to go to college, and a couple others I got *in* college I ended up givin' away. No kiddin'; whatever I's supposed to learn I didn't, cause the main canine chapter was yet to come; that German Shepherd on a farm east of Cincinnati, Ohio, starting in about, oh, 1987.

Almost all black with a few matching tan spots on her face, KoKo was stunning to look at, if usually on the thin side. I'd come in and find her food untouched most nights; but if I stayed to play with her, she'd chomp and romp too just because she was happy.

Happy or not, KoKo was one monster of a watchdog, and with an uncanny knack for picking out the bad guys: she hated cops and my ex-mother-in-law worst of all. Next in line was some ol' witch that ran the art gallery downtown who had the gall to ask me—in front of KoKo—if she was a stinkin' Doberman! When KoKo heard that, she liked t'a jumped halfway out the truck window, derned near vascsectomizing me a second time, trying to get to that ol' bag. You know what t'ough, it took her only one far off glance at my pre-teenage daughter to wag her tail. And I tell you this: they only saw each other once a year. That's a fact.

But now that goldanged dawg had an absolute love affair with cats. I never understood it. She'd spend hours prancin' from one end of a smelly ol' sofa we put out on t' porch t'other chasing some fool cat. Never once did she get tired of it. If she caught one, she'd trot all over the da'gone yard with that stupid thing danglin' outta her mouth, head completely buried and lookin' dead as a frickin' doornail, then drop it just to watch it scamper off with one of them dumb-ass spike hairdos you even see grown men wear on TV now. Down deep, I knowed 'em cats loved KoKo as much as the rest of us. God just programmed 'em not to show it.

Not included in that group of dog lovers were the locals. Country folks have a way of being neighborly all hours of the day and night unannounced. They say they're no accidents, and then, well, Kathy was always spewin' out some drivel about how she never knew what possessed me get t'at dawg anyway. But KoKo's presence did fix all that dropping in on me stuff. I got plum lonesome sometimes; hell, even Kathy stayed away now and then.

I guess Shepherds get their names honestly cause no amount of scolding could keep mine from tormenting my horses. Christ I'd get mad. If I ever showed the slightest irritation with a horse, KoKo'd charge in like a damn bull moose, creating utter chaos. Nor was that talent just applied to horses:

Early one morning she and I were walking through the fog coming off the "Uh-hia"* smack into a bunch of my neighbor's pigs. I mean they was right in my front yard! KoKo and I just stood there looking back and forth at each other three or four times in complete shock, till finally I said, "Shoo!" to them smelly things pigs. When I did

* Kentucky Speak for "Ohio."

that, that crazy dang dog jumped right in the middle, scatterin' them ignorant things all over the gol'dern county side. Chasing 'em up and down the hills, I kept thinking, "If only one of you- dog or pig- could unearth just one little white truffle !"** (I love'vim truffles, by the way even though I'm the only one'n the county knows what t'are though).

With degrees in music, it figures I'd have some goofy assed singin' dog. Why, shit fahr! KoKo's bark normally lasted a few seconds, then sustained to the mournfulest freakin' howl I ever heard. What's more, she taught ever' danged one o' her mates and pups to do the same idiotic thing. In the middle of the night they sounded like a German *Chor* of drunken wolves looking for a piece 'o ass in a' echo chamber. (I'm also the only one in the county knows what "Chor" means. C-h-o-r. It's a German word that means "chorus"). Lord, they sounded dreadful.

But now KoKo, she was 'right smart' o' strong and limber. I mean in her best years she could chase down a rabbit at full speed, hold the neighbor's pit bull down by the throat till I squirted water on 'em, and

*Gourmet member of the mushroom family, dug from the ground in Italy and part of France. Dogs and even pigs are used to sniff them out. They are very expensive, only available around December, and are, oh, so good!

even give good chase to tractors in high gear, one of which ran over her about a week after I got her.

She'd dash off on a damn dead run when I said: "KoKo, go get 'n the Truck." Once inside, like in about, oh, mid-August, she was happy only with that bristly-haired body stuck right up against me. I never figured it out, especially with the air conditioner clutch burnt out on that stupid rig ever since I had KoKo.

And her tongue would hang clean out from her mouth the whole time, slobberin' all over the danggum floorboard and 'em eyes and hers leavin' the road only long enough to look over at me as if to slurp and say, "Oh boy, Poppy! That was a leaf! D'you see that?"

When I wen' nt'uh hardware store, she'd slide over behind the wheel and sit t'ere the whole time like a' obedient long-eared chauffeur, teachin' t'people in'tuh store to howl in 'neir own right.

Lord, though, how that dawg could stink! The smellier things got the more she liked 'em. I'd like to a' fainted when she'd catch a skunk, or roll in cow dung or, worst of all, feast on some dead critter, then come up and lick me in the face when I wad'n't lookin'.

But now I tell you what, the feelin' I had watchin' her and Buck*
play in the snow after I'd come home from a hard day of strugglin' with
my tone-deaf students made it all worth it. That feelin' was as pure as
'ze driven white stuff itself. Once it snowed so high them dogs couldn't
even move in it. It took me two hours just to blade the driveway off
with the tractor. After I did, though, I pulled the car up on t'it; KoKo
and Buck chased each other 'round that banana boat for half a'hour, just
because s'ey could.

Now get this: they say a dog's lifetime is as long to them as ours
is to us. I just don't see how that could be. About the time you get 'dem
damn dogs trained to the way you want, why, hell, the're old.

Like KoKo, for instance, must 'a started slowin' down already
when she was barely eight years old. Usually pretty feisty, I noticed
she'd hang back at t'gate every time I let her and Buck out of the pen.
The pummelin' he'd give her if she ran with him was unmerciful, no
longer much fun. Sometimes he'd get all the way up to the porch before

*A companion I bought for KoKo

he even realized she wasn't with 'im. After he finally got the piss and vinegar outta his system, KoKo'd slink on out. She just wasn't herself no more.

.   One cold February night I think it was, Buck's hyped-up, lonesome journey started all the way back at the doghouse; KoKo didn't come out with him, even when I called her. Fearin' for the worst, I went to the house and came back with a flashlight and peered in. KoKo was layin' on her side, stock-still. I went and got the drill and took the front panel off and crawled in, the thought running through my head that this time she really had brought me my knees. Except for a little spittle oozing out from her gums, there wa'n't no sign of strain; but she was stiff all right. Buck had stayed with her till I got home, but it took weeks for that da'gum dog to stop charging back down from the porch to trounce on her when I'd let him out at night.

And my cheeks and my lips taste like salt just talkin' about it.

I loved Buck too, but after KoKo died I found him a new master. Some guy down county wanted him to guard his body shop; he wasn't even fazed when Buck charged him with his teeth showin' behind the window glass sitting on the truck seat. I pulled up the fence to the pen and burned the doghouse clean up and even cut down the trees I'd built it into. The grounds- and I guess my memories too- seem like they're easier to keep manicured that way. And I made quite a ceremony o' hauling off the gate: it was the only time I ever went to the Mason County Landfill with just one thing in't' truck bed. That gate was the front one, the one with the braces that spelled out the letter "K." KoKo died when she was nine years old exactly; she was a perfect "K-9."

I own that old place still, even though I don't get out t'ere enough to call it home. It's run down and nobody wants it. People out t'ere'd rather haul in a damn trailer and put in the front yard than do anything with a' old house or a big house. But, you know, I like to think there's someone watching out for me; I kinda, well, dream of rekindlin' things one day I had before, only, course, with a different ensemble, if you know what I mean. I'd say I'm halfway there, spendin' pretty good stretches agin innuh nice weather.

The old timers like to say that Kentucky grows rocks. Jesus Lord, it does look like it sometimes. Here an'ere, the ground down where the pen was 'll push up a piece of paddin', or part of an old boot. I reckon 'at's a good thing. I like having the little mementos; that way

I'm sure to remember my old companion, maybe… maybe even longer'n Buck did.

Bearing Interest On A Practical Family Savings Plan

I

The Mark of Ownership

Practical! That's what we have to be, and live according to our needs. After all, no one else will clean up after us. And hard! That is how we work for the things we care about, including our property. Land too is fair game, however we use it to survive, and comes under the bending sickle of necessity, to say nothing of the pride of ownership. It *is* ours, after all!

No kidding?

Consider this. Only God owns any land. Next in line, this particular part of the world belongs to the North American Native. The groups that drove him off formed a governing body that claimed a fragile ownership. Ever hear of *imminent domain?* It was that body's to give away, or sell. Besides, if we owned it, really owned it, would we pay taxes on it? Nevertheless, with an average lifespan in the mid-seventies, we humans are "bullish" as hell about what we claim to own.

Mortals are mere ships, moving through deep waters. They leave one shore and arrive at another, make their way against storm and calm waters, through both the brilliance of day, and night's murky uncertainty. They may enjoy the journey, simply borrowing a few things to use that they can't take with them when they truly go. Those beings occupy but a space in time, then pass it on, where or to whom no one is at all sure. In a few short years, few will remember.

Still, we self-appointed barons spend what feels like a millennium possessing property. Then, we pirouette; we sell, or die. Suddenly we've never owned anything. What a concept. Was it ever ours?

What we own is what we *do* to our little piece of ground; our mark, the one we leave behind. That mark remains for a long time, perhaps forever, which in fact, is the only way we prove any type of ownership. Those marks exist as choices, things we keep up with, or neglect. The responsibility for them is awesome, yet scarcely considered in our self-absorbed greed and possessiveness.

II

Outlasting Identity

Deeply considered, it is a fascinating concept that we—we who wear the human clothing—with our very hands can actually construct things that outlast us!

In a fair world, those items would either cease when we cease, or enable us to carry on as long as they hang together. The objects we assemble (buildings, crafts, even rusting machinery) are the comparative on-goers. While on earth, we pore over our creations as if a part of us, when what we really do is proffer them to a later time, to those both seen, and yet unseen.

The shelters that were standing when we came on the scene are, obviously, marks left by others in earlier times. They are part of our history, donating to us an identity, and telling us about the ones who made them: what they valued, how they spent a typical day, and perhaps even what they might have said. The objects are as close as anything else to the acquaintances with those of old that we have.

But what difference does it make? What *is* identity anyway, and why do we even need to know about our predecessors?

Knowing anything is justified by the feeling afforded having learned it; it is knowledge for knowledge's sake. Historical learning, that which gives a notion of what life in former times was like, may teach us just what "quality of existence" really means, as opposed to the plasticity of today's world. It can mean a deeper sense of self, a point of *human* reference, from which springs our own individual contributions. It helps us live—and die—make choices for the better, and toward fewer mistakes. While knowing something of the past may not change us at all, we can better know why it didn't do so.

People do not value their parents and grandparents only for the time that they see them physically, even though their relationship obviously changes once they pass on. Some immerse themselves in genealogy; others cling to the more intimate belongings of deceased family members. Some do it to excess. But, whereas it is inadvisable to become obsessed with the departed, it seems natural to not let go of their intimate possessions. Through them we continue to communicate, and to feel, probably in a different capacity from what we otherwise would have.

But, our emotional connections need not be limited to smaller or more intimate objects. They can be lavished as well on the grander, more traditionally impersonal examples of earlier handiwork, namely buildings, their furnishings and crafts.

III

In All Things Related

Consider a radical thought still: being all God's children, we are *one* family, not just separate biological ones. Since God loves each the same, we cannot be other than brothers and sisters.

All material possessions left behind, then, are those of *our* loved ones. It doesn't matter who made the things or who had them, or even whose immediate family they were; the important thing is that they were *someone's*. Those people constitute our family. They are actually….. "we" ourselves.

You can feel the family ties walking into an old house. There is an air about it, even empty, that is seeking to speak to you. Imagine all the babies that were born in those rooms, right there, many of whom died. Think of the people huddled around a fireplace, sitting on primitive chairs, or eating at (now) old tables. What did they say and how did they sound? Where did they fit into the changes in the sound of our version of English that letters sent back to England proved was almost immediate? What were their values, their concerns? Aches and pains? Their fears? There is a closeness beckoning to you.

Run your fingers across the nicks and scars of an old bench or dresser. You are connecting with the people who made those nicks. How did this gouge, this very gouge, happen? Who said what about it at the time, having no idea it was patina in the making, or that something like patina itself would even exist! How did the person who did it feel about damaging it?

One can't know. But in entertaining such thoughts you give your imagination a chance to do something for you. In all of art, there is something artificial, which is where the fancying comes in. The same is true for history in general, and its value as an endeavor. The imagination lets us fantasize and, thereby, elevates us from the humdrum of our daily lives; we "get away" in favor of something more ideal. We are improved—maybe healed.

IV

Maintaining Display-sure

You may not want to live in an old house or sit on furniture you find uncomfortable. No one's holding a gun to your head to do so. My father would quip that he wasn't interested antiques because he grew up around them. As products of our age, we are addicted to our own set of creature comforts. Even people such as I, who do live in historic homes, make compromises. Essentially, we must. But, by not using these things functionally doesn't mean we have to destroy them!

Even the hard-core, practical-minded person who says, "I'd rather live in a trailer than heat that old thing," or "I don't want that junk in MY house"…surely this person would notice a sad difference viewing a roadside with only trailer parks or houses from 1960 onward.

In making choices away from older surroundings, why kill them? Why tear them up? There is a broader responsibility involved than just to one's own self, or current property. If we own something now, then so does the world, and forever.

Objects of antique craftsmanship have the right to be seen. They represent a style that was harder come by, yet often superior to our modern contrivances. The tastes and costs of this age dictate that precious historical examples will never again be seen once we fail to preserve them. They are, as fossil fuels, gone for eternity.

Fortunately there are organizations dedicated to historic preservation. Our cities manifest the results. Specimens located in rural areas, however, are much more in danger. For most country dwellers, the property itself is part of the livelihood. There, one battles the elements to a greater degree. Blows dealt to farmers through the years are serious. That practicality dominates is understandable. Many country dwellers I know live from hand to mouth and maintain more than one job. A few even use old furniture and barn timbers as firewood.

The problem is that some of the most unique historic architectural structures (and their settings!) are in the country. Sadly, many are abandoned and falling- or under current plans for being torn-down.

As a second house, say on a rural property, a building may be an "eyesore" to you. But, it can be cleaned up! Hopefully, it will stand until you have the resources to make minimal repairs to keep it from disintegrating. If sound enough, use it for a warm-weather guesthouse. If you don't want guests around, leave it unfurnished. Just let it stand there, majestically, a great Phoenix towering from the ashes of history, and a memorial to those who toiled there. But please don't take away the culture, the variety and depth of human perception, simply for the sake of utility.

Smaller objects too can be admired without inconvenience. Using an old piece is the best way to preserve it. But, displaying pottery or furniture is also fine. Donating or selling it to sympathetic persons or museums is great. Or just protect it in an outbuilding, waiting for the right concerned party to come along. Do anything but make sinkhole filler of it!

Even for a country little more than two hundred years old, our rural areas contain unique masterpieces. American antiques routinely sell for higher prices than European ones. Attrition sees to it that the longer time goes on, the fewer are the things that survive. In arranging our priorities, we would do well to integrate the importance of the preservation of our heritage into our consciousness.

Doing our individual parts is crucial. Practicality doesn't have to reign supreme; it can co-exist. We can respect the past as we contribute from our own age. We have merely to think of those who will come after us: our children and their children. If we love them, we care about all that concerns them. We want a world in which they can be admiring and happy. Hopefully, we will give them enough variety and beauty for which to continue to think well of us, rather than a characterless globe, with which to be annoyed!

Myself Is Ashamed Of We: The Amateur-nouns Of The Pros

I've a knack for it; it's true, though through no particular self-styled virtue. Credit my mother, who put something out in the genes, also verbally rapped me across the knuckles when I misspoke.

My friend Michael's father, many years the archetypal stern school principal, got through in a more fiduciary way. He sat his sons at the dinner table, preparing to pay a nickel if caught making a grammatical error by one of the others. It was the same father who corrected the body-family's English at reunions, and wouldn't pay Michael his allowance–more accurately *wage* for hoeing the garden–if he discovered a single missed weed.

My high school English teacher sprouted from the same human weed patch as Michael's father. I seldom cracked the books in high school, normally making Cs and Ds anytime I needed to do so (study) to score well. Basic grammar tests were not in that category because of what I drank with my mother's milk; my teacher knew it too. I looked up once to find her standing over me as I whizzed through some pop pronoun quiz. When our eyes met, knowing I had not studied a lick, she growled: "The longer I read, the angrier I get," drawing out the words "longer" and "angrier."

Accordingly, though not the last grammatical word, I will usually offer up one or two of them so that everyone knows where I stand in the tropical storm that constitutes latter day communication. Moreover, something drives me: I have this wacky notion that people should speak their native languages well, and find the continual butchering of the King's English nothing short of reprehensible.

It is the butchers in the public eye, though, that annoy me most, and which I herein target. Since I sleep to the accompaniment of talk radio or Iphone podcasts, I am bombarded by the veritable stream of basic mistakes out of the mouths, not of babes, but speaking professionals: those whose general knowledge is much more vast than mine, whose approach is otherwise exacting, and whose tongues are crisp. Since I was clever enough to choose a profession that allows communication through musical sound, I am not on my own hit list; but myself is.

In contrast to what many seem to believe, by no means are all the aforementioned meat-cleverers American. The other morning on WOR radio in New York, I woke to the recitation of an email from a British woman that said, "Myself and my family will be visiting you soon." Of course, the show's host, Ed Walsh, whom I do like, once confessed that, "A living will would be good for Chris and I." It takes a strong will to be good for I.

During the twenty-five or so years since Edwin Newman's book, "A Civil Tongue" hit the store shelves, a craving for the word "myself" (extended to "yourself," etc.) has soared out of control; based on what I hear, it's an embarrassing obsession. We are too modest to say "I" or "me."

Myself's slip level at the time of Newman's volume nevertheless inspired him to entitle his last chapter, "Myself Will Be Back After This Message," alluding to the lingo of sports anchor Brent Musberger. Musberger's entire sentence had gone, "Phillis, Irv, and myself will be back at halftime." Thank God his real self would weigh in for reportage; couch potatoes hate having it phoned in.

What may have been a slip then is a slip no more. I hear the stupid word ("myself") on the street, in church, on TV, and from my waiters at the diner. Still, I believe the latest phase of the rage to have had its beginnings about ten years ago, at University of Cincinnati faculty meetings, where announced the Assistant Dean of Payroll and Finance to the assembled professors, "If you have any questions, stop by and see my office or myself."

"What is this, I thought, "a striptease?" With *my* salary, I had observed the inside of her office a number of times, never once, however, questioning a real bodily representation. Come to think of it, maybe it's why it never made a difference in myself's paycheck.

In all fairness to the assistant dean, such language was rooted, not in rolls of pay, but the rungs of academic toehold. Itself's lack of erudition, represented by the university-wide memos I would routinely receive, astounded me. Trickling down the "*Igitur*" handrail, our *un*-assistant-ed dean's favorite word was, "impact," used, without exception, as a verb. On especially good days, we were exposed to this verbal treat four or five times in one half hour of ourselves' meeting. Normally, I had the feeling clumsy verbiage only bothered me. But when the great white father announced a change in the name of the Alumni Office to, "Office of External Relations," the faculty erupted into a chorus of "boos." For once I was proud of the body un-politic. Still, it was shortly after that I handed in my nonlinguistic-motivated resignation.

The Myself Surge has gone the same curious route as the nominative pronoun one. Of the two, the latter is to me the more egregious error, requiring specific thinking. Even the normally well-spoken Marty Brenaman, Hall of Fame radio announcer for the Cincinnati Reds, says things such as, "Between *he* and" so and so, or, just today: "It will be good for Steve and I."

Why don't these guys wake up? Prepositions take the objective case whether another implied person is split up or not. Marty would have never said, "..good for we." I guess the assumed urbanity of separating plurality is just too tempting. There are too many people in a typical sports broadcast booth anyway. Besides, Marty is in the Hall of Fame. Good for he.

John Batchelor of WABC radio and beyond is, for my money, the best of his chosen profession. For one thing, he is too smart to allow call-ins. Why then, the other evening would he say, "Aaron, do you have anymore questions for John and I?" Question I, question I, for the commercial break is approaching!

With the literary equivalent of a deadpan expression, our beloved *New York Times* once quoted (the people of) the New York Yankee front office on the occasion of pitching coach Mel Stottlemeyre's resignation. Owner Steinbrenner (generally referred to as "The Boss"), through his office of media relations, said that he wished "he and Jean" the very best in the future. I was always proud to be a New Yorker, and Yankee fan. It takes a caring Boss, an exceptional media office, and a *very* savvy newspaper to carry through with such amateurnouns.

You thought I was kidding when I said "bombarded!"

On October 27, 2005 (pronounced "two thousand five," not "AND five"), a seemingly delightful young man by the name of Jason Tomlin replaced another apparently delightful young man as host of a country music program emanating from Nashville. In doing so, the first young man quieted several attendant rumors flying 'round Radio Land. Putting all possible suspicions to rest via one gross but all-encompassing announcement, he affirmed that indeed, "My wife and myself are having twins." Yikes! Myself is exponentially reproducing.

Ah, but the A+ gold star goes to one Dan Patrick, pinch-hitting for The Laura Ingraham Show. Referring to an ongoing rift with show host/political writer Bill Maher, Patrick said that since Maher had declined the invitation to slug it out on either of their *own* talk shows, certain people had sought to arrange a match on some neutral territory, with, "…myself and he." One stop shopping!

Here is the sad part: my grammar checker doesn't even underline most of the previous examples. What an age of supposed erudition we live in! Perhaps it is why such an Ivy League-educated specimen as Michelle Obama one morning a few years back over the CNN network said that what was, "…hard for Barrack and I." If such things are hard for she, imagine what living in the White House will be…like! Or such a successful figure as Don Imus, let us know just this morning that his group of seriously ailing children stay in his ranch house "with my wife and I." One can see why they call him the "I" man.

There can be little question that language is continually changing and ultimately made correct through usage. It has taken me, for instance, a long time to leave the single space now preferred by editors between sentences. But I have even heard linguistics teachers claim that rules are out and that only communication is essential.

Balderdash!

No wonder a friend of mine, she, who worked for a popular music video company, said that the younger crowd of employees was always poking fun at her for having the effrontery of speaking in complete sentences!

I maintain that usage alone, especially that born of ignorance and stuffy, trendy jargon, is a lousy way to keep the path to communication alive. As long as the rules themselves are spelled out in the books, I think some form, to go along with all the content, cannot but be a good thing.

Why shouldn't we dress ourselves up verbally the same way we press our clothes ourselves when the maid is sick, or, "of" a Saturday morning, ourselves wax the automobiles? Don't you yourselves enjoy a little exercise?

Change, like peace, doesn't begin with myself, but with me, even as I speak. If mere usage is the paddlewheel of animate language, each of us can and needs to make a positive contribution. Kindly help me stand on my own without myself.

Clear Sailing And Omelet-Present Danger

I was already over that part, all the patterns and the creature-of-habit complex. The trigger was my closet. It's draped like a swamp oak with stuff I'd pass over each day for the same old sartorial affronts. From there I started to see that things like eating Cuban every single New Year's Eve was, after all, rather strange.

Oh sure, I know. I still breakfast at the same dive. The waiters plop the decaf on the corner table, head for the kitchen with the spinach omelet order when I hit the door. But that's just ritual fluff. I mosey down the same side of the street, grab a *Post* at the usual stand, cross Broadway catty-cornered at 83rd. No big deal.

What woke me to the real danger was all the gear-head talk about "South Beach." Body fat being illegal anywhere near Greater Miami, the last thing I'd have dreamed of was a weight loss diet by *that* name. All I did was have this nightmare about Versace, the ultimate walking breakfast target, and bolted upright from a deep sleep around 2:00 a.m.

I mean, I'd already been torpedoed by motorized wheelchairs, moon-walked by swinging backpacks, and nearly decapitated under a storefront scaffold. The tire prints left on my new sneakers—some delivery kid going the wrong way—didn't do much for me, though the scab from my free ear piercing did: compliments of an umbrella mushrooming from a subway entrance, it summoned my doctor from *his* deep sleep: my blood iron level was dangerously high from all the spinach!

Still, something was in the air.

My stroller pals (you know, "The right to roll supercedes the right to exist") normally wait to assault me out in the open. But just the other morning, this twin-kid killing machine bashes me in the knee before I even make it out of my courtyard. Fleeing the scene for the federally secured safety of a bank, this homeless guy manning the door blesses me out for not tipping him, and trying to then get around some virago doing a big arm-swing number, I catch her fist in just the right place to emasculate me when she suddenly darts to the side.

On Ash Wednesday I wasn't Catholic. Just the same, Luigi the Squeegee thought he'd use his wiper pole to show the faithful cueing up at Zabar's what I'd look if I were. Dodging him, some kid starts referencing the size of my manhood when I question him for smacking me in the gonad with his tennis ball, and ducking in the back door of our building, the neighbor's Wheaton Terrier—ecstatic to catch me outside the confines of an elevator—uppercuts that same spot with her left paw.

In other words, what had taken me a good six months to get me more or less screwed and tattooed on my otherwise harmless way to breakfast was in "Total Eclipse," being nailed, flailed, assailed and impaled in a matter of about six days.

*

God knows I hate to sound paranoid. But *Murphy's Law of Pain* dictates that if you have a sore body part, anything that befalls you always does so on that spot. And since my hernia surgery, I'm, well, touchy. This epididymitis is killing me.

If you're a male, the epididymis is that mass attached to the top of your testicles. It connects to a cord that sends up those squiggly little things that get you a lineage. Being surgically altered, they simply get me clogged and inflamed. Normally you don't know you even have an epididymis. If infected, you don't know much else.

Here is something you don't want to do with an inflamed epididymis: stand up. You wouldn't step off a high curb, drive bumpy roads or let yourself flow, freely "dressed" on either side of your inseam. Sex is okay as long as you go at it like a ninety-year-old geek, but long car trips are out of the question.

What *is* recommended is 1) drinking a lot, 2) wearing brief-type underwear three sizes too small, 3) picking soft-textured pants, 4) being a couch potato and 5) moving ever so gingerly when you can't stand the confinement any longer.

Okay, so here I am at vacation time, the ever fidgety, "Type-A" me: can't run, can't jog, can't very well play around, can't pilot my new tractor, even if I vaporized myself to the farm. I can't go walking around New York, cause the locals get *their* knickers in a twist seeing me reach down my pants to adjust myself.

Mercifully, some deity points the way: a cruise. It was brilliant. Ship sails to Bermuda out of New York Harbor, leaving me no lower than mid-shorts by the time I get down there in a cab. Glide along like on a waterbed, lounge around sipping piña coladas, levitate to the upper deck on the aft and stern elevators; even do the Jacuzzi, as long as I step in while still sober enough to tell where the jets are.

In truth, it was the perfect invalid vaca.... well, except for one day at sea.

Though the sky was clear, the wind was dress rehearsing the 16.3 hurricanes due to strike the eastern seaboard over the next two years. Having to support both me and "myself" along the ship's padded hallways, I reaffirmed things like the need to recline whenever possible. So, since the shape I have always left a hotel bathroom in for the maid is important to me, I also deemed it prudent to take a seat to pass water, even flush from there, given the difficulty I had coming to an upright bodily position, even on *terra firma.*

My thinking was mostly good. The flush mechanism, located at the back of the toilet, however, was difficult to reach from a sitting position. Plus, the atomic blast a ship toilet makes—just when you think it's not going to this time—is nothing if not terrifying at close range. Remembering my young daughter's Mr. Rogers song she used to belt at the top of her lungs about going down the drain, I deemed it wise to reassess my position.

The next best thing was to only partially rise, moving slowly and carefully, enough to reach the lever from a semi-crouched position. But the toilet top, leaning against the back still, blocked it, so that I had to tilt the lid forward to get a grasp on the flusher. There would have been no problem with any of this, you understand, except for leaving the *ultra painful* part of my anatomy dangling precariously from between my legs.

Enter the devil.

Spying a couple of unusual objects flapping in the breeze, he decided to rock the boat at the very moment I finally managed to flush. The rolling of the vessel, coupled with the mid-air position of the toilet top, sent the latter to a most emphatic forward whiplash, drilling its edges into the upper, therefore hideously afflicted, portion of my inflamed testicles.

But the fun was only half over. An agonized reaction to 1) the movement of the ship, 2) the toilet top slamming down on my balls, 3) the bull elephant rifle crack *it* made being reunited with the rim, and 4) the underpinning of a pair of velour sweat pants, lined with briefs small enough to fit my youngest grandson lying around my ankles—all these, I say—sent me, in perfect theatrical time to the delayed detonation of the maritime flushing system, careening into the shower, on a ship only two feet away anyway, spawning, as it were, lying spread eagle with this flamingo egg plastered to my forehead, a NEW Bermuda Triangle.

*

But the break had been just what the doctor ordered. Tripping the light fantastic across 8_4_th Street my first morning back, I felt like Ebenezer Scrooge after the transformation: the azure-clad street crews that demolished me with their trash-wheelies were *charming* fellows. The thousand-decibel blast from a set of air horns pulverizing my eardrums barely elicited my glance; and donning a pair of wrap-around

Foster Grants healed my burned retinas from the new Broadway "Walk and Wait" lights. As for the stroller chauffeurs usurping my innate right to the sidewalk mini-ramps, the darlings returned my blown kisses with the gusto of a gentle stock who can truly tell where they're going, and, at the same time, care.

Indeed it was a new breeze that brought me to my little coterie on that cloudless day, confirming what you hear but well nigh never believe: you get back what you send out. The owners let fly their "Hi, Mr. Gary," with special fervor. The cell-phone battalions ended all calls; even the chef came out for a hug.

As the book says, "It's all small stuff." Freed of Erroneous Zones, I've empowered myself to *choose* happiness, found an eternity within, and *love* the new Yanni CD I bought on the boat.

Still, the sweetest treat of all was watching my favorite waiter faint straight away: instead of the spinach omelet, I ordered my very first ever.... **Eggs Florentine!**

November *Attacca**

Summer has gone, the leaves fallen, caught in the vortex that is the New York Experience. Though it matters less; the morning sojourns having turned uptown, closer, and uneventful. Our timeworn restaurant has lost its lease.

On this day, I, however, chase a hare of a different Westside fur—the Midtown New Balance store—and chance by the old haunt: abandoned, un-swept, soap-marked.

My outreached hands support a flattened nose against the rain-pocked plate glass, as the eyes set my mind to musing: Mike and Joe are beyond the partition, staging a comeback. The dust bunny, faintly scooting about the floor near my old table, was there all along, playing peek-a-boo as I munched my omelet, even on the day they told me about a plane several blocks down, strangely unable to miss one of the tall buildings.

Zigzagging past the bleached oak frames, I fondle the tarnished brass doorknob my hands helped make that way, and smell—I would swear—the chlorophyll-less imprinted ledge, where leaned the daily special board. About my feet, a wind-swept pile, as if anchored by the dinginess of my sneakers—shiny white for the cruise—sings an Auld Lang Syne before the landfill.

Dejected, a glazed look on my face, I store the store of memories, resume the uptown trek, somewhere mid-thought between what Longfellow called "My Lost Youth" and the comely figure sauntering ahead of me.

But before reaching, even, a single mini-ramp, a rather normal-looking man—brownish red shocks from his face and bare headed—leaps with antelope-like strides from before the comely figure, shoves an orange but blank sheet of construction paper into my face: "SIR! HOW DO YOU DEFINE FURY?" he shouts so closely the hairs of my nostrils stiffen from the off-road diesel quality of his consonants.

A surprisingly graceful right *relevé* brings me even with the face belonging to the comely figure.

"Now there's one for you," opines the askance eyes, lips belonging to the face belonging to the figure.

"First time I've been asked that today," I hear my own orifice rejoin, though in the depths ponder a superior response:

> *For I know wherefore Fair Fury sleeps:*
> *'Tis but one wee groin uppercut beneath my layers.*

Thomas Wolff was wrong once more. I am home again, and all is well.

Taking One To Know One To No One

He died last month.

Who, you say?

Well I don't rightly know. He was rather short, slight of build, and had worked in broadcast and print media. His interests seemed to have centered on things like health food and investing, also panning for minerals, and even singing on occasion. Oh, and he was my mother's brother. But I don't know who he was.

The man it seems strange to call my uncle gave new meaning to the term "loner." In my whole life I only remember seeing him on three occasions, albeit one of which was an extended visit, but the other two of which were funerals. My impulse is to say that no one knew him, at least, well. But then, I was one of them: one who didn't know my uncle well enough to even say that for sure.

When my own brother was making his first attempts at talking, he dubbed my uncle, "Unkie." It stuck with my sister and me too and, I must say, handily so. For instance, when you called and blurted out, "Unkie?" he could narrow the caller down to three people on earth. It was convenient for everyone, so much so, in fact, that I really should have tried it over the last forty or so years.

But I didn't. Our last verbal exchange took place just after my grandmother's funeral. At the time I was still an undergrad; retirement for me now looms in the not too distant future. For the major part of an adult lifespan I had no contact whatsoever with my uncle. It wasn't as if we had words. We in fact didn't have them, because he obviously didn't care to, and I responded in—or should I say *without*—kind.

When his mother died, Unkie behaved pretty much the way he did before his father's funeral: he had one ten-minute period of absolute and uncontrolled sobbing, then regained his usual, and equally absolute, reserve. The only punctuation of his otherwise pervasive remoteness was an occasional violent outburst, just to scare hell out of us kids. He scolded me for slouching, said he didn't frequent places like pool halls, corrected my spelling of "facetious," slowly shifted to second gear *after* turning Minnie Grave's blind corner, and uttered the one-syllable sentence, "M'some," when my mother queried, "Brother, do you go to church?" But that's about all there is left of him for me.

For years, I wondered if my uncle was keeping a dark secret: he was a NAZI spy on the naval destroyer he served on in World War II. He was a gay man from a time and background that made him unable to deal, loathed it and never acted on it, which is why he didn't marry. Or he did act on it, which is why we never saw him. It was perhaps just too odious for the much-traveled gent to be around the country way we talked, or its equivalent brand of Christianity that surely suffocated him growing up. I don't have a clue; my one remaining uncle didn't call and it runs in the family.

I thought Unkie was in an assisted-living facility these last years. The truth is he lived alone in a tiny trailer he rented for two hundred bucks a month. We were told he could have bought the thing for a measly thousand, but declined. He took long walks, garnered the admiration of those he did meet, and, for sure, consumed tons of peanuts: the hulls covered the floors of his two rooms like the pub whose doors he would never have darkened.

And he wrote. My uncle wrote volumes. He may have had a typewriter, but I'm guessing he spelled most of his thoughts out by hand. Though a man of decent means, the years had turned his native conservatism to miserliness. In the middle of a record Arizona summer heat wave, the air conditioner wasn't even on where they found his body; the papers—strewn over his bed—had kept him cool enough. I didn't know any of this; it was as if he and I didn't have phone service. Only.... only I'm not a miser.

Since no one knew him well, no one knew what he wanted done with his remains. My sister, the good one in the family that way, had at least stayed in touch. Her name on a sizeable savings bond was one of the few indicators of what my uncle's wishes were with respect to any part of his estate, or for that matter, what he thought or felt. Though I didn't know him well, I know now I should have called anyway. Much more than something left to me, it would have meant a great deal to *him*: Unkie appreciated what he wouldn't bring himself to do.

Personally, I think he planned on living forever on those dried fruits and nuts. Then again, maybe he just didn't want a crowd of people sobbing over him for ten minutes when he went. In the case of the latter, he got his wish. What's left of him lies in an urn in a hole in the ground, next to the parents he was not that close to and in a place he didn't want to be. His funeral and burial combined amounted to a prayer and two scriptures, accommodating a grand total of two people: one read and prayed; the other dug the grave. At least I *think* that's the way it was. I, well, couldn't make it. It was kind of far and, you know...

Ironically, the last feeling I remember having had for my uncle was one of anger; anger because he never contacted my mother. That was, oh, a year after *their* mother's demise, the apparent precipitation of his longest disappearance. But then, time and Unkie's final event seem to have softened me. Now I have an emotion that doesn't do him *or* me any good. I'm sad, and wish I could call him.

The almost twisted upshot to this—more than one man's—tale is that I too should receive something from him. Entered against the red-ledger side of my own periodic financial issues, that very intelligence triggers two new, two *very different*, feelings from the one I had all those years ago. And I'm having no small difficulty choosing between them: happiness and guilt. Or is it avarice and unworthiness? Puzzlement, or merely that viscerally hollow, creepy way you feel when someone close dies. Of course, it couldn't be that last one; we weren't close. No, the uncle didn't call, but if the nephew had, he might at least know what to feel now.

Believe it or not, the old fellow once indicated that he really should have been in touch. Again, it was about my mother, pretty much mindless her last years, when she died. Typically terse and media-voiced, to my sister he managed, "...I think of the times I could have written, but didn't; when I could have called, but didn't."

You'd think that reflection, as if rolling off the chemically etched templates of a lifetime, would make me feel better, since he didn't call her *or* me. But it doesn't, especially since there was no particular reason for either of us not to. I mean, I guess I know that. I never stopped to wonder if he liked me or not. Maybe my challenge is just accepting that our family doesn't have that many *close calls*. Well, most of us. Come to think of it, I don't really know that either. If I live to be even older than my uncle, I'll never stop shaking my head at how things change; how they go 'round then come around, hit you differently. Like the words to that old country song I used to laugh at, and that now goes through my head in another way: "If the phone still ain't ringin', I guess it still ain't you."

He died last month. The name was Lynch, age eighty-nine. It was in a small town, not far from the California state line. But I don't know who.

The Vast Left Lane Conspiracy

What is it, a magnet? So many bad front wheel alignments pulling that way? A sexist thing, you say; how about a failure to understand basic signals of the road, plain English, oh, or talking on the phone?

A teenager, I was in the car of a friend who was pulled over for running a stop sign. The trooper proceeded to explain the complicated thing about stop signs: "You see, you come up, and then.. and then, and then you stop; after that, if clear, you proceed."

Those obtuse upright things with printing on them, usually on the right side of the road, are calling to you: the ones that say, "Keep Right, Except To Pass." Parsed, they mean that normal interstate highway driving is done in the right lane, and that the left one is used when overtaking another vehicle (meaning car or truck) - only. Also the ones that say, "Slower traffic keep right."

You see, these signs are especially important when there is another vehicle to the (your) right, preventing passing in either lane, so that you need to turn your steering wheel (that thing hopefully in your hands) in the direction of your right arm, which is that long object dangling on the opposite side from your left arm. As a young friend of mine said to his mom on a rush hour traffic backup, which she was causing, "Mom, you should get over." Replied his mom: "Why? I'm going the speed limit."

Would she or any of my readers care to know why, now? Because you are a clog; something that blocks the flow of traffic, causing a snarl, otherwise known as a slowdown, traffic jam, or grid lock. You see, when there is a car on that right hand side of you (n...n...nearest your right arm), there aren't any more lanes on a normal interstate, maybe even city expressway.

All this has nothing to do with how principled you are, how fast the person behind you wants to go, or whether you agree with his speed; those are none of your business, as any cop in the world will tell you. Your responsibility is to get out of the way. Especially if you are the first in a long—or short—line of cars in the left lane, it is imperative that you, 1) slow down and get over, 2) speed up and get over; not stay in cruise control, not stay within ten miles of the speed limit, or make any other philosophical statement or gesture. Oh, and the flashing headlights from behind that puzzle you? They're vehicles too; their drivers want to wake you up and send you (over, maybe to the moon) where you should have been all along, only now much more emphatically so.

The above emphatic part reminds me of a story told to by an acquaintance of mine who teaches **English as a Second Language** to adults. My acquaintance wanted to show the class the movie *All the President's Men*, but thought she had best go over some of the film's verbal phrases in advance. One such phrase was "Fuck off." Asking the class what it meant brought on a lively discussion that resulted in everyone's pretty much getting it.

But then, one pensive student in the back of the room wanting to take it a step further, raised his hand and asked, "Can one say "fuck off" nicely?"

A second member of the class proudly thought she knew the correct response: said the second person when called on, "Please fuck off?"

For what it's worth, here is what someone who drives fifty thousand miles a year (me) makes as one of my main rules of the road:

that no one EVER has to pass me on the right on an interstate highway. Mostly I am successful, and on the rare occasion that someone has to flash lights to get around me, it takes only once and, at that, I am annoyed with myself.

For the life of me, I cannot understand that anyone who has the basic intelligence it takes to pass a driver's exam cannot comprehend what I am saying, much less be angry with me when I am trying to get around his/her particular vehicle by merely hanging behind, let alone flashing headlights, or even honking.

So, dear friends, buddies, and darlings: here is a kind piece of advice for all potential bleeding heart left-laners: if you would like to help prevent at least half the traffic snarls in this country, possibly the entire globe, unless you are actively overtaking another vehicle or preparing to turn left from the same lane in a very few seconds:

GET YOUR FREAKING ASS *OVER!*

Otherwise, please fuck off.

Teaching From the Inside Out

You're a voice teacher.

You live and work in the great metropolis of New York.

New York: The City That Never Sleeps; the haven for the arts, the musicians' Mecca, where anything goes between 9:00 am and 10:00 pm, even in your own little cubby hole.

You therefore have to be *imagining* your cubby is turning into a hotbed of harassment; merely dreamt that this conflict is your new and private little piece of hell, hounding you till you're driven from the building, the profession, maybe your right mind.

As with all other private music teachers, you're subject to the vicissitudes of freelancing in the urban setting. You make your living taking students' word they'll show for their sessions, with no guaranteed institutional paycheck and benefits package. But those irritants exist across the board. You have it worse. In your case it's the great mass of sound coming from both the piano *and* singers' voices— those are just getting warmed up after the first hour—that set you apart.

There are people, you have chanced to learn (the hard way) who interpret this loveliness as *noise*. Accordingly, you feel beads of cold sweat upon your forehead as you impart the hard-hewn gems of wisdom, knowing how fragile the security of your little fortress—a laboratory for the improvement of your own performing art—truly is.

Your wonderful next-door neighbor of many years, an elderly lady who welcomed the music as companionship, passes on. Until then, you have greeted her warmly, done odd jobs, carried groceries, and bought vitamins. Bless her soul, she was even known to complain that you weren't making *enough* music.

But her inevitable time comes, and the landlord's agents begin desecrating her refuge so soon you imagine their having been perched outside, ready to move in for the kill. At untold levels of decibel, they wield their sledge hammers and air drills. They smash and crash through the winter and into the spring, sending you to the brink of insanity. As the calamity moves from demolition derby to sheetrock showcase, you grow more and more on edge for the ones who will take her place.

And, boy, were you right!

*

There's this curious thing about apartments: people have the habit of living in them. "Living" can include breathing, walking, talking and, horror of horrors, making music. *You* understand all this, but your new tenant pal may not.

If you've been living right, your new neighbor will fit the image of a good ol' boy; or someone who works late and visits an out of town lover on weekends. But get a skinny-lipped duo from some sleepy New England borough, into, say, twenty-four hour transcendental meditation, ceramics, silent movies, or muffled nocturnal culinary affairs and you're screwed! Plus, according to the wording on your lease, there may be little you can do about it. One day you're all warm and cozy inside your own miniature castle; the next day you're out of a job.

Would that you could interview prospective neighbors! The "quietness-is-next-to-Godliness" types would be spotted at a hundred yards. They're mid-to-late-fifties, wear gray-green every day, and *always* carry an umbrella. They majored in library science or work as curators. Their facial expressions remind you vaguely of being force-fed a turd, their head motions that of a bird of prey you saw diving into a piece of last week's road kill. But, alas, this subject doesn't add up to a popularity contest, and renters have no co-op/condo board.

An open-minded person, you're pardoned for your naiveté, assuming the afore-mentioned vocations engender interest in other branches of art. It'd be just peachy, for instance, were you a home-based karate teacher, tap dance instructor, or chain saw sculptor. But, musician? Are you kidding?

In your stymied response to the new neighbor's protest, you promptly soundproof-padded, carpeted, and moved your piano to another room, separating your art from the neighbors by some three walls. Mercifully, this procedure reduced to a reassuring nil the sound, even inside your *own* apartment. The cost of the small-scale construction need not be sweated, nor the number of lessons it will take to come up with it! You colleagues remind you how lucky you are, merely to have solved the problem.

Never mind, too, your having heard nothing by way of complaint for the last month, assuming the issue resolved, only to return from Thanksgiving vacation and find a pre-eviction letter from the landlord's lawyers taped to your door. Brush quite aside the fact that you've now retained an attorney of your own to the tune of God knows how many more voice session fees.

Let your Melatonin, your Ambien, then your Xanax, nocturnally assuage memory of the goon beyond the demising wall's subtle first protest, presented in ghostly form before your entranceway; he who laid siege to your doorbell on the opening page of your first singer's first aria, after a rejuvenating summer in the Rockies.

With a dismissive flourish of your high-wristed pianist's right hand, you wipe from your mental palette the complaints of these ingrates with every *fortissimo* your singers now let fly, or the tendonitis from the subconsciously tense underplaying of the accompaniments-especially since the neighbors above and below, whom you truly love, have joined the party.

Your seven-foot model "B" Steinway grand, now only one room away from its location thirty days ago, suited them better where it *was;* they now risk your long friendship by timidly broaching the subject. One, whose shrink office is over your new studio, listens to her patients spend the hour obsessing on your singers like the mother they could never forget. The other, a lovely person and even music lover, wonders if you could think of a mode by which she could sit in her living room in the evening without wearing earplugs.

Noise, you say, is a natural part of life in the inner city. You're patient about it when the 300-member-plus-Great Dane clan upstairs barks, rolls the family bowling ball, and activates an in-home airbag testing device at 4:31 every morning, trying to interest someone in going for nice Central Park pee-pee. So, why can't the people next door indulge in a little realism, for Christ's sake?! This is…………………………… **NEW….YORK!!!!**

In the midst of the fray, you show signs of paranoia and other instability. You see your now *reptilian* neighbors at the local video store and wonder about your life-long commitment to non-violence.

You start obsessing on the possibility of your beady-eyed landlord's personal involvement. The new neighbors have mysteriously not only discovered that the two apartments were originally one unit, but taken up again with a former friend (a specialist in pre-Inca tapestry weaving), who happens to be looking for—guess what?—an apartment! You calculate the avaricious owner's pocket being lined by your eviction, your rent converted to a welcome mat for your successor.

What before you could only vaguely imagine, now gnaws at you every waking moment. Feeling your life being yanked up by the roots, you consider your options, since private teachers, after all, are loaded with them. You can 1) stay where you are but rent a teaching studio, 2) be employed by an opera company or school, 3) even move away and leave the business altogether. You've considered it in the past anyway, every single time, in fact, one of your singers gives you the shaft.

But wait. Renting a studio skims your income right off the top. Teaching in a school gets tedious, what with the pompous, self-serving colleagues, and in an opera company, you have to prop up all those high-maintenance singers. You want something more creative. After all, you are a teacher in *all* its various manifestations. Besides, you can't quit now. You only recently paid off your education!

Though you bitched, you muse on just how good you've actually had it. Private teaching does have its rewards: inspiring all those young minds, or shaping someone's initial concept of a composition, all the time staying in touch with the great musical masterworks. A good shrink could help deal with all that singer nonsense.

"Okay," you say, reaching for your cell phone. " I don't know. Maybe I'm just......"

"Uh, hi, *Un*-Real Estate?....... Yeah, I'm looking for a rental, couple of bedrooms or large living room, good fire walls, hideously lonely or deaf neighbors on the road to living forever, Upper West Side; you know, legally guaranteed I can make all the racket I want in a unit that hasn't tripled in price over the last twenty years. Oh, and with a long lease—for about a thousand bucks, okay?

"Hmm?   What?...Dreami...........Whattayuh   mean,   *that* Unreal?.......Fort Washingt...? You mean Valley Forge, but what's that got do wi…..……Y…………? No, I'm not that old, but…. Yeah… Wul… Really? …….. Yeah..   …… Uh-huh….oh….okay…. …. Mmmm, well… Yes, yes…. Sure… Yeah, I will… Yes. Nice talkin' to you too."

Again, the Voice

This chapter is dedicated to the memory of Michael S. Kavalhuna, who died following a severe bi-polar episode. I loved Michael like a son. He was one of the best students I ever had and, I must say, whose singing I was able to affect the most of anyone I taught. I wrote, then read, this semi-poem at the end of his memorial service in New York City.

We called him The Voice.
His was the voice, not always of reason,
Sometimes one crying a little in the wilderness.
But it was The Voice of sincerity, of integrity,
And of consideration; The Voice of well-wishing,
And of innate kindness, to you, and to me.
He was Michael, one of the greatest guys you will ever see.

You would hear The Voice on a stage or in a hall,
Or wafting from a bathroom stall,
It sawed through the door of a practice room,
And melted your heart, since you knew from whom.
And you'd hear it in a church, as if from a steeple,
He was Michael, one of the nicest I knew
From the ranks of people.

More than once The Voice filled
The corridors of a hospital ward,
Just because it could.
As long as a heart beat in the body,
You knew it would.
And it was heard from a patio in North Carolina,
Singing to a brother, or to friends,
To all creatures, great and small,
They were his universe, God's concert hall.
He was Michael, the most inspiring people I ever taught.

And The Voice shot up an elevator shaft,
In a building in Manhattan,
Though you were on the ninth floor,
Behind two closed doors and a batten,
In between, it even showed up on my answering machine,
Ornamenting to vocalises higher and longer,
Just to let me know the audition couldn't be stronger.
He was Michael, one of the considerate ones.
He comes to me in a dream, or by something he said,
Arguing basketball, though it was my team that led,
Or from a message in my mind, ending with all his numbers
Just once more time,
As if I didn't know them all by heart.
Or was it from some piece that he sang?
He was Michael, of purest The Voice that ever rang,

When I was a young singer, an older colleague shared a secret:
He said he always tried to sing in such a way that the conductor
Would think of him if that work came to mind in the future.
There will be many a baritone song like that from now on,
For me and, I dare say, for you.
He was Michael, a memorable singer
Among the ones I knew.

But he comes to me in another way.
He is the little house finch that pops on my window sill,
Or under the air conditioner in the studio still,
And says, "Gaowy! Gaowy, down here.
Look. My tongue….! It's relaxed now."
My raspberry friends play with me like that all the time,
As if dress-rehearsing their tricks sublime.

When Michael stood by my piano doing the human things,
He was as unimpressed as all the rest,
At a finch earning its wings,
Not even then did he know he was on his way,
Whether singing to God or the MET Judges' nod.

Now, he lets me know he understands these wings things
We take an interest in growing older.
When the lessons don't go as they did from Michael's folder,
He   sends   me   patience,   or   a   prompting   word,
I can always tell his chirping, a way of singing for a bird.
He was Michael, one of the sweetest chirpers you ever heard.

And so on and on he chirps, and sings, and floats,
A little stuck in all our throats,
And in our collective ear, our sight, our mind, our heart,
Too dear from us ever to depart,
Still, just beyond the reach of our outstretched paws,
Join with me now, one last round of applause.
Whatever year, whichever cycle;
He will, forever, be our Michael!

A Finch In Time Saves Mine

And an Ode

Waiting for the muse put me in some pretty good company.

I remember that piece of Russell Baker's from the 1970s, written during a touch of writer's block. He found his topic—the block itself—in the eleventh hour, thereby avoiding the suicide window one more day.

A woman with my Kentucky Zip Code once asked some party guests to bring lists of topics her husband might write about in his columns. It was a stroke of genius. The-by now-ultra famous name was Clooney, and I think Mister must've written about all of them, *including* the party.

My subject this morning derived from, well, a more natural source.

I sat in my New York apartment, itching to put finger to key. When my wandering eyes reached the open window, what should appear but an adorable male house finch, checking me out from atop the air conditioner? With twisting little jerks about the head, he chirped,

"Gaowy! Wite about me! Me and awl my bwuddies. Will you, Gaowy, pwease?"

Well I was off and running! Not just saved from the window, but back home in Kentucky, wearing what Arlene calls my "farm face." And remembering.....

Roger Tory Peterson's description of the male house finch had stuck, and I began to wonder about all that could go through such a splendid little head. It must have been an hour I sat there, critter-musing: By which instinct do birds mate only with their kind, and why do they have specific nesting habits? If you put a certain kind of house on a somewhat distant a pole, what lures martins-and *only* martins-to it? Why does a killdeer dig in the ground, or a chimney swift—the "cigar with wings"—set up for a good smoke in a flue? What did it do before chimneys? And why on earth would a finch pick a big city apartment building when it has the whole natural world at its feet?

During the 1970s my classical singing ambition consumed every waking minute. I thought all the fuss my friends made about their animals was downright silly. Today, with tears over my own pets much more recently subsided, a chance meeting with almost any great or small creature brings me to my knees.

But the *animal magnetism* was really in the genes. Dad liked kittens and Mom peppered the house with bird images; when the snow flew, she tossed scraps to the real ones. Purchasing my first farm in 1986 was like looking into a mirror, taking in objects not allowed recent right of passage by my ego.

And how fascinating that property was! Every year it produced things I never saw before, or would again. A pair of American kestrels took twelve years to materialize, then multiplied and moved on. There was the Carolina wren that popped up on my patio, minutes after the good Mr. Peterson had taught me what to look and listen for. A bluebird and a house wren played together so joyously in a tree beside the house one year that they sent me looking for them with my morning coffee. But, alas, the orioles I kept my eyes peeled fifteen years for never appeared. Last spring, they were everywhere.

And they came in numbers. Our German Shepherd had something like sixteen pups in one litter; nobody could get close enough for an exact count. Oh, and Mom's blood surged when I caught sight of a V-shaped flock—lumbering too low and sounding too strange to be geese—approaching my house. No higher than watchtower when directly overhead, their folded in-flight necks told me they were....***blue herons.***

One especially fine day, a herd of about thirty white tailed deer *dashered* and *dancered* up the valley behind my house. When I screamed in amazement, they scattered to all points on the compass. Weak-kneed from the excitement, I pivoted for the porch. Yet by the time I got halfway, they had *reined* themselves in for a spectacular reprise, gliding up and over the road fence like so many dreamed-of sheep, and thundered back down to the sanctuary of the creek bed. It had all come and gone in about five very surreal minutes.

In my day I provided lifesaving hydrotherapy to a half-severed leg of a mare, body bandages to a chewed up colt, and even sex guidance for my stallion's first love feast; and I do mean guidance, his initial attempt having landed him on the ol' gray's broadside. Frankly, I thought it a helluva way to achieve birth control, but a friend, watching the whole thing along with my father-in-law, summed it up better. "Hell, he didn't even buy her a drink," he quipped.

On a stormy **April 15th** night of some year, I arrived home in business suit to be greeted by a different greatly agitated female horse: "*COME ON*," she urged, running from one end of the barn breezeway to the other. Without changing clothes, I raced to the outside door where I pulled a brand new chestnut filly, alive but helplessly stuck, out of the mud. After cleaning her off, I bedded the two of them down for the night in the dry safety of a private stall. It was a seminal day for the baby's first colostrum cocktail, and we named her "IRIS" as an offering to the tax gods.

When Kathy's cat died, I too cried like a baby. The little pillowcase he slept on by her head every night ended up his shroud of yellow. The last time I saw it, it was all stuck with—instead of the Shakespearian "yew"—the moistening tears of a near-mother as she comforted him one last time in the grave I had dug that morning. To this day I use some version his four-letter name as my passwords.

Before long though I was cat-laughing again, this time over a new mamma that plopped her eyeless babies in front of some July 4th partiers, just to show them off. I found a half grown male cat nursing with a brand new litter of his part-siblings, and was entertained for hours by the 70 X 70 wild kittens that ventured from the safety of an old deep freeze to perform the evening's feline Marx Brothers routine on the patio furniture.

But then I cringed at the skinned baby rabbit they amused themselves with in the barn, and the myriad half-eaten trophies they would bring through the pet door for us to step on barefooted first thing in the morning.

And there were nocturnal guests besides my neighbors: coyote packs in the night, and in-house raccoons greeting my return from a summer in Aspen. Mostly I was impressed that the discombobulated creatures had trekked to the toilet bowl to first wash off the food they stole from my pantry before dining.

In fact, since the people on my road had assigned me the appellation, "The Educated Guy," I thought it appropriate to open the manor to all *manner* of varmint entertainment. Accepting the squire's invitations over the years were chipmunks, mice, vicious stray cats, black snakes, *faux*-imported ladybugs by the millions, birds, and even a New Year's Eve *Fledermaus*.*

But this, *this* was life in the country and I did love it. I could write the definitive Beast Book, accounting for what seems a lifetime of still more memories: the wild dogs that drove my horses through my new fence; the only owl I ever saw, inspecting my midnight firewood gathering; the feline demolition derby my darlings made of the upstairs bathroom hearing the veterinarian's voice; heads of reluctant baby barn swallows peering over the sides of their generations-old nests; "Gerry," the mewing mamma of them all, hysterically scaling the library ladder when I practiced my opera arias; and the hundreds of unidentified sights and sounds that would go on and on and on in the inexorable chain of "terranean" existence.

Fledermaus is German for "bat". In some parts of Europe, especially in Vienna, it is a great tradition to perform Johan Stauss' great Operetta, Die Fledermaus on New Year's Eve, often taking the house orchestra seats and concluding with a great ball. It's especially exciting in that in the act where there is a ball that is part of the story, certain singers show up to favor the guests. In the case of a great opera house like the Vienna State Opera, it is traditional that certain current and well-known singers are invited and "show up". Though I could never get tickets for the occasion when I was living there, I remember hearing a recording of Vienna Staatsoper (State Opera) in which Joan Sutherland and Jussi Bjoerling were two of the surprise guests. I have goosebumps just remembering and telling about it.

Yet......... none ever touched me more than my fine-feathered raspberry friend this very morning. So from one awed, to one owed an ode:

Thanks, little finch, who but for an inch,
would have flown in my chamber and been
nevermore welcome than a raven.

Thanks, little finch, who with this flick and that flinch,
could snap up a bug, or but be scarfed by a lawn-meower.

Thanks, little finch, who in the clutch and the clinch,
saved me from the window you navigate so effortlessly:

Do come again one day,
But, if in a pinch,
With birding so busy,
Then send Mrs. Finch,

She's almost as pretty.

You soar the heavens,
You fly so high,
You'll meet my mummy,
Way up in the sky.

I think you'd be chummy,

I'd say it's a cinch,
And I'd go with you too,
But we'd need a winch,
To float as you do,

You   sweet   wittle   Gwinch,

So say "hi" from Gaowy,
Oh, Mom's name is "Lynch."

Refluxions From A Gut Level

Preface:

Reflections: It has been an ongoing theme, both comically and seriously, the metamorphoses that have characterized my life this far; and I have addressed them accordingly. One thing I have probably hammered at is the importance of history: political, yes, but also all kinds of art, the development of which depended on that history. Medical science has fallen into line as well, and when it and art intertwine, each is made more significant exponentially. Furthermore, when something, even something outmoded, is more effectively pointed out with the aid of an event or other illustration (in this case, a chapter) the jury can comfortably rest. The time span from which I have chosen elements of this book as a whole is bound to come to light in historic stages too and, reflects research and technological advances. My awareness has changed, while some of my beliefs definitely not. I have always been an unwilling researcher, and there are issues in these chapters—as much memoirs as anything else—that have undergone technological advancement since the original time of writing. That the glimpse into the past justifies itself the bringing to light the place this particular one holds, is clear, if for no other reason than that a remedied solution of today was not often the case earlier.

Refluxions: If you were a pianist you'd have tendonitis, if a violinist, bursitis. Singers forever battle congestion. So goes the way our bodies respond to our psyches. We weren't born with such responses, but took to them like termites to a woodpile.

An astrologer recites the symptoms under your sign. Immediately, you think of some instance in which you conformed to every one of the characteristics. Or thumbing through a medical encyclopedia in the morning, you remember having had a touch of half the diseases in the book, and may truly come down with one or two by nightfall.

I went to school with a kid my friends had fun with; if we told him he looked a certain sickly way, he'd leave school in a few hours complaining of the symptoms. As products of "New Age" reasoning, we wonder little at the notion of thinking a condition into manifestation.

Still, I doubt we go so far as to consider the sheer *popularity* of a disease, or notice that once one is discovered, everyone starts getting it.

Mononucleosis was out of control in the 1960s. Perhaps *one* of my students came down with it in the last fifteen years that I taught. Ulcers were big for years, but no one seems to complain about them anymore, conceivably due to medical advances alone. But, every ambulatory human being in the world had hypoglycemia in the late '70s and '80s. Now, doctors tell me, the AMA scarcely recognizes it except in pre-diabetics. Others say that "pre-diabetes" is not a term should even be used. Some repetitive motion supersonic condition was bound to hit the scene when "Blackberry Thumb" was the rage, and although I never had one, my iphone has to be a major cause of my carpal tunnel, now enjoying an hourly visit all the way up my right arm. I guess it took the place of TMJ, the non-slack jawed disease of choice a short while back, now coupled with another TM-something I more often know more about than doctors I have mentioned it to. Whereas allergies persist in today's singers' ranks, they hold a poor and distant second place to— you guessed it—gastrointestinal reflux.

People have often struggled with conditions, too, for which they had no proper title. Take maladies of the stomach, probably the most frequent *locale* of physical complaints. Those ailments are referred to alternately as indigestion, heartburn, gas, sour stomach, dyspepsia, bloat, *agita*, something not agreeing with you, and 'bellyaches'.

My ex-father-in-law used to say, "Something I ate didn't drink." But what would *he* know? He broke the Italian law by refusing to eat garlic! Two things gave him *mal di stomaco*: eating and not eating. When I suggested he see his doctor for a little Zantac, he replied, "Nah. They'll just want to give me one of those upper GI things." The human animal wants to go on suffering indiscriminately as *well* as **inarticulately.**

They nevertheless came up with remedies. Many were, in fact, good ones. Arlene says that even while growing up, she saw the bed of her grandfather (known as "Honest Abe") elevated at the head for his stomach problems. Chiropractors rail against that it for the health of your back. It may be like taking ten pharmaceuticals for the contraindications of the first five.

Yet, it is unlikely the grandfather, before retiring, spoke intimately to his wife of sixty years of the need to neutralize the acidic contents stemming from the diminished lower esophageal sphincter presenting with his congenital hiatus hernia.

"Honest Abe" Lincoln was another grandfather type. Referred to as "The Ancient" by his staff, he is supposed to have continually slept sitting up. When Mary found him thus propped up the first time and remarked upon the curiosity, I doubt that even the well-spoken former country-lawyer responded, "I'm sorry, Mother, but those damned Domino's Pizzas ooze fourscore and seven burning beads of duodenal contents over my *Squamous Epitheliuma*!"

My wife's grandfather also took ginger ale and chicken soup late at night to soothe him. For my father-in-law it was ice cream. These remedies point up the importance of alleviating the psyche more than anything else.

From a medical point of view, minor stomach problems almost inevitably have to do with acid control. The carbonation and fat found in the above foods constitute modern day 'no-no's' for bad stomachs. No doubt their benefit lay in doing what *any* food does for a few *minutes*: neutralize the acid temporarily. Both Honest Abes and my ex-father-in-law were assumable fast asleep by the time the acid took over again. A few hours later, they may or may not have had their sleep disturbed. However…..they didn't have to SING.

Unknown until recently, what many, if not most, minor stomach "complainees" did have had was gastrointestinal reflux disease, or GERD. Partly because it now has a recognizable name, reflux is for sure the current rage. There has been at least one television commercial in recent years singing the virtues of a chewable reflux remedy, and someone recently told me about reading an article on the subject in a flight magazine. That's getting there.

But, considering how widespread, and, more to the point, poisonous it is to the vocal cords, reflux seems to have been little more scantily treated literature on singing and vocal disorders! When it *is* mentioned, the information and its remedies were outdated. Many singers—and teachers—consequently are still in the dark about its effect on what they teach day in and day out. Humbly, I leap into the edifying breach…

The first published medical results regarding a connection between laryngeal problems and reflux came in the late 1960's. However, it was not really until the late 1980's that laryngologists' "refluxive" attentions kicked into high gear–a long medical incubation period for a condition that was to achieve such marquee status.

There is even a good chance that *you*, reader, have had the condition without being able to call it by name or knowing that you have it. Not everyone displays the same, or the traditional, symptoms. Still, the common ones affect over sixty million people in this country alone. Sixty per cent of all people experience 'heartburn' (essentially, reflux in action) at least once a month.

Singers who have the energy to get by without eating have it good. Norman Treigle was one. I was told that Samuel Ramey's wife would take food from him sitting at the dinner table. French art song specialist and teacher, Pierre Bernac said to me once that he was *never* hungry, even during World War II, when there was almost no food. But these are in my experience exceptional singers. Most singers' tendency toward "pigging out" doesn't just have pictorial outcomes.

Though otolaryngologists have long since zeroed-in on reflux, its causes, and manifestations, singers may still get the same perfunctory assembly-line treatment that suffices for all other people. As advised to me once by an otolaryngologist, *"A singer should find an*

Otolaryngologist (ENT) who is oriented toward singers." Nevertheless, a few short years back, I was often surprised by the number of working vocal professional performers I talked to who had never even had their vocal cords looked at.

For the average 'Joe,' mild-to-moderate cases of reflux are simply annoying. For singers, they are disasters for which standard medical advice will probably not suffice. And I am further surprised at what I have heard from my students and see printed in singing-oriented magazines, supposedly by medical professionals for avoiding the consequences of reflux. The recommendations might be sufficient for "regular" people. Not so for singers.

Here is a typical scenario: an active performer, you never liked to eat a lot before you sang, even a rehearsal. You were nervous, plus it was not comfortable to breathe on a full stomach. Eating before, though, would have been preferable to what you ended up doing. After rehearsals or performances, hunger rears its ugly head. Rationalizing your need for fuel to keep your general energy up, you eat, and, perhaps, drink alcohol. Knowing also the need of a good night's sleep before the next day's agenda, you do what is the worst thing: go back to the hotel and straight to bed.

Hopefully, your moment of discovery will not, as it was for me, be in the middle of a performance. Although that experience is what it took to finally get me diagnosed, I could have done without the trauma. I had dealt with the annoying symptoms for most of my life, hoping to just "sing around them," all the while getting incorrect information from medical advisors. But then, I had never been vocally annihilated by it until it took a sudden turn for the worse, probably coincident with my becoming older.

Prior to losing one's voice almost completely, some of the telltale symptoms can include: altered speaking or singing voice for no apparent reason; heartburn; actual discomfort in singing; awakening in the night (or morning) with a burning, or mild choking sensation from which you may have difficulty clearing your throat; a "lump in your throat" or difficulty in swallowing; frequent need to clear your throat or cough; sour breath; stringy mucus, repeated burping or hiccupping, or mild nausea, and even a feeling of overall congestion or sore throat. Drastic alteration or loss of voice after singing a few minutes is probably the most perplexing symptom.

The more acid that is secreted in the stomach, the greater the stage is set for reflux. At these moments, a slight amount of material flows up the esophagus, at least far enough to travel down a canal formed by the bottom of the arytenoids leading to the vocal cords. When it goes that far, you often cough, which helps. But, if asleep, you may and may not cough, which is worse still. Of course, if you are lying down, gravity is on reflux's "side," not that of your vocal mechanism.

Vocal damage from reflux can be immediate, though the recovery time from it is less determinable, particularly when its buildup is cumulative. Singing in this state of irritation can exacerbate the problem, as well as contribute to technical (vocal) problems due to over-compensation.

A doctor may see the following: red or spotty-red vocal cords, particularly posteriorly; swelling in the same general area; a darkening of the red color, particularly at the bottom of the arytenoids; rough or bubbly skin, uneven edges of the vocal folds themselves, thinning of the vocal mucosa, swelling of the vocal folds, improper depth of the vibration and, in more advanced conditions, contact ulcers. Your dentist may find decay, particularly at the back of the mouth, along the lower gum line.

A percentage of people actually "reflux" in an upright position, which may account for some of the long-presumed allergic reaction to food. Most of the damage, however, is done at night. Although doctors are not in agreement, the presence of a hiatus hernia must certainly be a factor, and people with reflux disease may be prone to pulmonary issues, including asthma. In extreme cases, the esophagus is partially eaten away, which can be related to at least one form of cancer, or at least its pre-cancerous condition. You could say that singers' symptoms can be a preventative mechanism for something more serious that non-singers would not have.

The stomach can normally tolerate its own acids without itself being consumed or bothered. Other body parts are not so adept. Rebounding from an episode involving mental performance-related trauma is especially tricky, complicating most singers' already conditioned fears of sufficient vocal stamina. I know; I am one.

Who could have detected how much Honest Abe Lincoln's problems had to do with political anguish, especially the loss of American lives in the American Civil War. Links between psychological factors and reflux is an area that *has* been studied. Dr. Deborah Rosen has written a book called "The Psychology of Voice Production," devoted to the subject. Not only is stress alone a factor, but physical-stress positions in connection, such as, even, driving a car can be problematic. Indeed, anything that decreases the effectiveness of the lower esophageal sphincter control, such as pregnancy, strenuous exercise after eating, and even certain forms of singers' (physical) vocal support. Other (mostly abdominal) issues, smoking, over-eating, and excess body weight, are known to cause an increased likelihood of reflux.

What can you do on your own?

Even for a singer who doesn't feel he/she has the condition, the recommended dietary remedy is not far from what is recommended for good health in general. I have read that as many as fifty percent of people who use their voices in professional ways show symptoms of reflux. To follow a severe regimen, one has to be willing to sacrifice. As I am often heard to say, such measures mean giving up everything that is good to eat and drink, and fun to do. Demonstrating my current age, one learns quickly why being spanked and sent to bed hungry as a child was such an effective parental punishment.

For starters, eat smaller, more frequent meals. You have perhaps heard (even by doctors) to allow two hours after your last meal or snack before going to bed or even lying down. Verily I say, if the time period since eating is not *at least* three hours, you may as well have not waited at all, and the poorer your diet is, the longer that time period needs to be. Elevate the head of your bed (so that your **torso**, not just your head, is lifted) six inches unless it causes problems with your back. Change your diet to high fiber/low fat, including lots of fresh vegetables and non-citrus fruits, and take over-the-counter antacids. Be patient. Lose weight (if appropriate), and dine in a relaxed frame of mind.

There are doctors who rightly insist that reflux can be treated by diet alone. However, the majority now prescribes medication for acid regulation. In the dark ages of the condition's history, antacids alone were the oral medical remedy. Next, it was the acid-controlling Zantac and Tagemet, at one time the most widely prescribed drugs in the country. Now the prescription group of choice is the stronger, different acting (and expensive) Proton Pump Inhibitors, such as Prilosec, etc. These are now available over the counter, though from time to time one there is bad press about being on them long term. As with almost any drug, the possibilities of side effects do exist. At best, though, these drugs essentially mask the problem, which is essentially a mechanical one.

Foods that cause the largest secretions of stomach acid are, logically, the ones to avoid. Most doctors put fried or other fatty foods, tomato-*based* spicy foods, citrus, alcohol and caffeine at the top of the list as culprits. Important to eat in moderation also are oils and spreads, nuts, chocolate, pepper, conventional salad dressings, onions, and anything else that noticeably bothers *you*.

Oh, and pray or meditate a lot, and try not to be fanatical to the point that you no longer have a life! Of course, no one ever said singers had normal lives anyway. So, while we're at it, don't travel, eat, drink and sleep on the road or have performance nerves. Train yourself that food is not recreation, especially now that everything fun to eat has been taken away from you anyway. Come to think of it, eliminate hunger altogether. It's bad for your health.......

Taking Leave For My Senses

We're not, I tell you; can't be. Even from one minute to the next, we're simply not the same. If the cells of the skin replace themselves, so it goes with the rest of us, our organs and brains. When we breathe, we reinvent, unrecognizably, even to ourselves.

Likewise with what those organs sense; if they—therefore we—were the same, we'd view things identically, year in and year out. We'd never grow, happily trudge on with the same mates, never find fault, and stay in one location. We wouldn't have much need for breaks and leaves of absence, or any other shot in the arm. Automatons, we'd be; not people. Trust the great French poet, Rimbaud. Said the *maitre*, "No matter what happens, no trace of now will remain."

Have someone tell you something you said years back. You deny it because you can't remember thinking that way. You're right; you are not that person. You read something you once wrote and are astounded to have even *put* it that way. Correct again, and because you are not *you* anymore. A distant prank, or the way you treated someone when a previous tissue mass governed you causes to you cringe, and you argue it *wasn't you.* It wasn't. We don't *really* evolve; we get reborn, though not in a baptistery. Otherwise we'd even look the same. Check your photo albums; is that you?

When in New York, I was one animal; in the country, quite another. How I processed was altered by what I saw and smelled and tasted, and what I otherwise did at any given moment. When I sang or taught, I was an animal all right! Yet, when gardening or mowing with the tractor, the thoughts that went through my mind could only have derived from a different DNA.

And, ah, when with my small grandchildren, I was another ineffable sort. And why not? They didn't even know my real name; to them I was, "Grandpa Farmer." I rest my case in the imbedded genius of the little person juror.

Michael was the one who told me know that God had a lot of fun creating me. I think he was right. The often "I" goes crazy without breaks. "It" strings out odious tasks, flits from one occupation to another, and doesn't concentrate well. The senses fry otherwise. "It" is too many and must go in search, reflect on who it really is (whoops, was) in any segment, how that particular "it" progressed from an earlier one, while moving to the assured next.

Nor have I come up with an answer that attaches to what is commonly called stability. Just ask Arlene if I ever do. Why? Because I am never me long enough to conclude: which one of me thinks? Which one feels? Which should I lay store by? It is not right or left brain, but *different* brain, so that the answer alters as I do. How, then could I expect to give an un-waffled response? Even con-joined minds don't think together.

Since moving to North Carolina from New York City a year ago, I have mused on why I am grouchier than before, when one would think it would be the other way around. I should have read my own book again, I would have known why; the answers were right there (Oops, here). I have lived all over, but my two favorite *sitios* were opposing each other: Full city and full country. Of course: I am schizophrenic. How could I fail to see? Here, I am in between, neither country nor real city, and reading this book reminded me of how alive I felt years before, how INTERESTED I was, how much more energy— physical and intellectual—I had and...and....that I miss both of them (don't tell Arlene). And I am not much interested in travelling anymore. Maybe I will in a few minutes; it's like the weather: wait a few minutes if you don't like it.

*

Before my first sabbatical leave at University of Cincinnati, that "me" was stark-raving mad. Everyone hears that teaching is high-burnout, and I knew why. Even though my colleagues had taught for longer than I had, I felt every inch of their burnout for them. I was nonpareil; possessed of a distinct set of professional criteria and sensibilities, of which I don't think my colleagues had a single clue.

And I still have that feeling, only then it worked against the "then" me. I saw through the nonsense around me to the point of thinking my own profession stupid. My normally low bullshit-quotient was maxed-out, and I even questioned how much I cared about my students, or the value in what they were doing in such a field.

I'm told that corporations are now allowing sabbatical leaves. Doing so, they embrace that which is hush-hush in academia. Leaves are instruments of rejuvenation as much as scholarly advancement. They are periods of healing, soul-searching, skin shedding. The provost knows it too, but can't say; the CEO can. Sabbaticals are times to take up something new, rediscover the "you" you had lost, or find the new one.

With "the me" of the time, the break worked. But then, guess what? I was a different organism, a foreigner unto myself. At taxpayers' expense, it was then I learned that I like to write down thoughts, even for circumstances in which a piss ant could plug in an article. But I didn't care.

A fairly common-occurring "me" is one who knows, uh, knew, he could put words together, but didn't do so unless petitioned. My singer friends would ask me to write their bios; when turning out university reappointment recommendations, the scuttlebutt was how well-written they were. Why the surprise, I thought. Wasn't it an institution of supposed higher learning?

During my sabbatical, whether or not I was any good at writing was well-nigh immaterial. I had found a project for my psyche, if one I could not report on to the dean, as required by school bylaws. What mattered, sitting on the back porch of my Kentucky farmhouse, was all the previously referred-to miniature 'buddies' about me, and mentally hugging myself for this or that clever thing I thought I had just written, then roaring with peals of singer-like laughter, all the way down the valley to the Ohio River.

A drunk, you see, had started a small newspaper close to my farm and invited me to contribute. It was the reward for having hauled his printing presses in my truck from Cincinnati. But I should have supplied the guy with Vodka as well. The paper folded after a scant six editions, as the sabbatical drew nigh to its *Sabbato;* the resumption of school soon loomed.

*

The significant part of my leave of absence was that, after only a year, I began to look forward to something that approximated work. Imagine my discovering a feeling similar to the one I had when first starting.

I was inwardly excited and, as much as anything else, the realization was creating a minute stir in the minute-man who always said he didn't want to live for his work; that his work existed because *he* did, not the other way around. No job was ever going to rule that "me."

Who was that masked man, that creature going around spouting things like, "While work may not have been the only thing to live for, there could be worse objects around which to center a life." Was there Vodka left after all?

Or: "Self-fulfillment, spiritual peace, and overall happiness are the qualities universally sought by adults. Mistakenly, we look outside ourselves for answers, when the key lies within. We're empowered to select, to choose our internal-eternal kingdoms." The university position need not have been previously blamed; it was all in how I dealt, how I perceived it! These were lessons like none of the previous "MEs" had ever demonstrated.

And in writing: "With time on our hands, things that go bump in the night crawl out of the woodwork. A few months have made me realize that I missed the challenges of school. I've acquired a new attitude, which, like everything else, has been spawned within me. And that "me" has begun with thoughts and words, which are, after all, prayers." As we think, we are; as we view, we do. It's amazing what you can learn from who you once were:

"A satisfying job can actually help make your fulfillment easier; it is an instrument, a tool and dye company, a medium through which we apply what we have already created. Since we get back what we send out, the enrichment is redoubled: the job is...well... a self-fulfilling mission."

And, finally: "My advice is to rehearse positive affirmations re your work and your colleagues. Speak these aloud and often. Remember the Seven Dwarfs: "Hi, Ho, Hi, Ho, it's off to work we go. "Hi, Ho is more than a soda cracker; it's the key to your true Ritz."

I was psyched. Coming back would represent opportunity, grounds upon which to prove; a lab for my words.

*

The students were the same, my colleagues ever small-minded. I had lost a crop of good singers, but it's the price of taking sabbaticals. The stupid university things: the illiterate memos, the politics, the dean's constantly employing verbs as nouns, and all the committee nonsense were soon as tedious as ever.

Ah! But there was the new me to deal with it.

Faculty feuds, long forgotten, re-ignited. Always the one to keep my colleagues guided through what was previously established, I saw what had gone to hell in a hand-basket in my absence. Factions were out of control. Talented people I recruited to the school were rejected out of hand. Those I resorted to sneaking into the school by committees

I sat on were the best recruits of the year, and I literally thanked God for my new "dealing" tool.

*

This great rejuvenation lasted for about a semester. In a short twelve months I was completely over the nonsense I had sprayed about when apparently desperate for something to occupy me on my back porch. Singed from head to toe, my molecules mutated yet again. Like a blacksnake, I had only an epidermal layer to counter the ones in the grass, my colleagues. I went from "Hi Ho, Hi Ho, It's Off To Work I Go" to "Ho Hum, Ho Hum, I'm Off To Work And Glum."

And so it went: the advancement of the "me," onward and upward. Or was it sideshow?

*

Motivational seminars and forward-thinking churches like to tell the story of a fellow that died, and when he did, went to a wonderful place. He was greeted warmly and taken to his comfortable, no-worries quarters, while kind people were his constant companions. In short, he lacked for nothing, until, after a few days, began to get bored. Attempting to wait it out, he only grew more restless, and asked the overseer for a job to help make him feel worthwhile.

But the overseer replied that working was not allowed there. The man responded, "Well, I'm accustomed to contributing, doing something to, you know, make a difference. If I can't, I may as well have gone to hell." Replied the overseer, "Well, where do you think you are?"

Yeah, well, I know what the thus-far progressed me would say to that:

"WELL, HELLO, HELL! Point me the way to the beach and send over the lime-slitted Coronas! I'm in for the duration."

"Well, for a while anyway..."

For Sale By Owner

It is time; time to move on, grow another skin, hatch from a different shell. The property run down, the trips taken too much out of me; I have done my part. Though like offering my heart and soul for a price, I will it to better karma and new blood, especially that which is more keenly endowed. With luck it will go to a nice couple from Florida that will invite me back whenever I want.

To the Editors: Please run on the weekly special and the Advertiser.

With regards,

G. Kendall

Ad:

The joys of country living and connecting with the past abound on this old Kentucky home. Situated on 11+/- hilltop acres and within easy day-trip distances of the famous horse country, bourbon distilleries, Lake Cumberland, Red River Gorge, Shakertown, and the urban centers of Cincinnati, Lexington and Louisville, the home features exposed beams, large spaces with ten-foot ceilings, the original cooking crane, and ten rooms total with operative wood-burning fireplaces.

Dates engraved on the house's hardware are from the mid-1850s. Yet research indicates that the structure existed earlier. Simple Greek Revival and "L"-shaped, an original double-roofed rear porch was positioned to take in a gorgeous- and to this day totally unspoiled-tributary valley with the Ohio River as a backdrop.

The exterior brick walls of the house are three courses thick, interior either two or three. Inside also are all the dog-ear moldings, pine floors and mantels from the day it was built. One slightly smaller bedroom has been converted to a large second bath. It is equipped with claw foot tub, twin sinks, utility cupboard concealing a washer and dryer and, of course, a fireplace: beyond its rear wall, the slaves' quarters.

The dwelling is in good condition and ready for immediate occupancy. It has updated plumbing, insulation, a 200-amp electric service and renovation throughout with an eye to both modern comfort and historic authenticity. There are four bedrooms, living room and dining room, keeping room, sitting room with library ladder, chandeliers or ceiling fans throughout, and a beautiful cantilever staircase. Any one of these rooms would work well as a fifth bedroom.

The charming and family-oriented river town of Augusta (five miles away) boasts a number of local luminaries and historic sites, including the very spot where Stephen Foster wrote part of *My Old Kentucky Home*, and an excellent restaurant in one of the oldest buildings in that part of the state. Without knowing it, millions have glimpsed Augusta's beautifully preserved Riverside Drive in movies, now a favorite sunset stroll way, antique/art shop center and boat landing- all within walking distance and plain view of the only Kentucky-Ohio ferry east of Cincinnati.

Twenty minutes in the opposite direction is the larger town of Maysville. Maysville has an historic district close to the river, with steepled churches and other aged structures housing banks, homes, shops and even the local law enforcement! Up "The Hill" is a more modern section, where one will encounter excellent shopping, franchise eateries, veterinarians, a good hospital, and an excellent community college. Washington, Kentucky, a scant mile beyond Maysville's southeastern city limits, is one of the most history-documented and quaint towns in that part of the United States.

Companion to the featured house is the nicest barn in the area, a stone-faced concrete block building with three stalls, county water, sixty-amp sub-panel, and a poured-floor work/tack/feed area. It is a solid structure that could easily be converted to a garage, pool house, or even guesthouse, and offers a view of the valley's lush foliage from the most striking vantage point on the property.

Tucked among the eleven acres are a pond, several hundred feet of board fence, stone-terraced herb and vegetable gardens, corrals, perennial flower gardens, a stone patio with steps and matching barbeque grill, fruit trees, mature shade trees, berry patches galore, and a Swedish-inspired outdoor dining area, all overlooking what many consider the most beautiful private view of the entire county.

This is a property of different looks: from the road a majestic and towering affair, from the front a modest plantation. On the opposite side, the landscaping and terrain combine for a sloping domestic charm that is special. The location is great, the neighbors kind and generous.

Taxes are extremely low for the property and for the county in general. There is another beautiful 36-acre parcel available nearby with barn, fence, creeks and county water. Both are for sale by the owner himself, who is willing to consider financing and/or renting-to-own. More photos are available.

Showing Up A Minstrel Show

"Waffle Show" would be more like it: she loves me, she loves me not. That is my singing life; that, and, "I love you, I hate you. I love you." Nor was it just because of reflux. A junior high baseball player, I wasn't as smart as Michael, who, getting smacked in the face with a grounder, dropped his glove and walked off the field for good. I was great one day, terrible the next, but kept on trucking.

Being first a musical instrumentalist too, I brought to the table certain charms, lacked others. Previously noted, I could count and learn music. But as a stage character, one who oddly enough, had not even tried out for the high school plays, I had a few things to attain. Still, as long as the director didn't ride my tail, my personality eventually took care of most of that.

Anytime I had to hang tough, though, I usually hung out instead-usually to dry. An askance glance would bolt me into the realm of self-doubts; shrinks weren't "in" the way they got to be later on. Some of my friends in the '70s did EST, but I didn't want to be what I called an "EST-hole."

The stock I came from was humble, the skin thin. My basic vocal sound was always good, though for a long time not large, so that I wasn't exactly comfortable *in* that skin. And speaking of "in," that's what Indiana University almost did me (in).

It was that school's heyday of renowned talent, as personally vicious as it was good, which included the teachers. Five years it was I spent, fighting my way to the academic/performance top. But even during such regrouping, I'd head out to my teaching job in Louisville, KY after a hard lesson of my own, swearing the entire hundred and ten miles that I was quitting.

On to the Curtis Institute of Music in Philadelphia and the family threads shown bare. Also previously noted, a few singing competitions led me to a good artist management, and I was beginning to turn some heads, at least until succumbing to my little Swedish distraction.

People who knew me in the early days use phrases like "raging young man" to describe me. Last time we talked about it, Janet, in all her goodness, laid most of the problem at the feet of my background, at direct odds with my goals. Being an accountable personal type, I was never able to pass it off that easily.

In the early 80's, my blonde girlfriend and I finally blew ourselves to small fragments. That took a while to get over, as did reviving the level my career had been before the blow *it* suffered staying too long in a country that offered little to foreign classical singers.

Plus, my management made a couple of significant mistakes. After I auditioned, the considerable powers-that-be wanted me for the remake of Barber's ***Anthony and Cleopatra,*** enough to offer me my *choice* of roles. The so-called high level management turned it down for a lousy thousand-buck Rogers and Hammerstein concert already on the books with the Milwaukee Symphony. Plus, the office never did anything with the prize I took in Geneva; inexcusable for a respectable management firm.

Returning from the land of clogs, I still had a few bookings with what had become of Barrett Management since the death of Lippman. But, the main body of my work for the rest of that year was a string of *Messiahs* with a neighboring state symphony. The orchestra had been on strike, though, and it was difficult to ascertain whether I would have income for the next months.

I didn't hear and didn't hear. I called the management office and they couldn't tell me anything, for the main reason that they handled the conductor too. Before resorting to waiting tables or unemployment checks, I decided to find out something from the orchestra's own office. Pretending to be calling for tickets, I included a query regarding the soloists' names. The name of the bass-baritone was definitely not mine.

In a rage, I called the replacement for Lippman—who, by the way would never have tolerated such a thing—and was connected to a junior salesman handling the gig for the final tell-all. The conductor was having an affair with one of his players. Her husband was a bass-baritone singer. To vent their guilt, they ran him in as the bass soloist, the renegotiated contract between the symphony, the union, and my management making it all possible.

That's when I began searching for a teaching position, ending up, oddly enough, with one of the best ones in the country. I wish I had starved instead. The politics of performing never prepared me for the politics of teaching. Although I did some very good work as a teacher and singer/teacher, studio rivalries saw to it that it was seen as an aberration, and I eventually moved on.

Through it all, my singing deteriorated from reflux, as well as from a great disillusionment in the world—moreover the *business*—of singing. Nevertheless, in the preceding years, I had been practicing the vocal repertoire that I always thought I would grow into if willing to take the time and effort. It is an issue for certain types of classical vocal-personal types. A singer is an athlete whose best bodily advice is to wait longer and aim higher, but like so many other things, is not in line with the plastic, "New York Minute" way of this current planet. Teaching had given me something to do while biding my vocal time, and it time it took its place—and a toll.

Reviving my interest in active singing was partially a result of Arlene's comment to me anyway. We had met at the Aspen Music School in 1993 and in '94 did a demanding concert together to good acclaim. Her reaction was that I should be singing much more, a collective word similar to "drink" for an alcoholic. I started learning larger Germanic repertoire, and traveling to New York on weekends to see her, rehearse, also do some private teaching. It was fun, but I gradually began experiencing discomfort after singing for a few minutes, though not so much different from previous experiences; I didn't give it much thought.

In the middle of it all, I was invited to sing the role of Mendelssohn's Elijah at my alma mater, the University of Missouri. It is a role that I was never sure my voice would be high enough for, but since doing the other new repertoire, I felt it was in line.

Wrong again! I could negotiate the part if in excellent shape, but the tendency to lose my voice after a few minutes went to a new level during the second half of Mendelssohn, and at the place I would least want it to: the scene of my first two degrees.

I was devastated. I had never had a truly bad experience in a performance and, all the way back to Cincinnati, pounded the steering wheel of my poor little Ford Probe in frustration. An ENT told me that I had four classic reflux symptoms, although the treatment didn't cure everything: to this day I have nightmares over my one and only semi-*Elijah*.

With discipline and medication, my voice got better, then, with advancing age, worse. The performance of a recital in the Big City music school I did was mainly to prove that, training like and athlete and living like a nun, I still could deliver. The concert went decently, but frustrated me all the more by my contracting a respiratory infection the night before, so that I couldn't be as free as I wanted. Too, I began to develop a more or less chronic bronchitis, felt terrible for over a year and decided to throw in the singing towel. I was later to learn that the reflux had complicated my ability to recover from respiratory infections.

When the condition got to the point that I couldn't' enjoy life in general, I went for the surgery. The technical term for it is *fundoplication* and essentially consists of wrapping the bottom of the esophagus with part of the stomach, after shoving a couple of organs out of the way. It is done laproscopically nowadays, and the surgeon, probably after spending a childhood in front of a million video games, needs to have practiced on a hundred poor living souls before getting to you.

The final regular chapter to the waffle story is that I was burned out on singing, teaching, and music in general, so much so that I never gave my voice a fair chance, once recovered from the surgery. To be sure, I was at the age in which most people don't sing well period, and was much happier now that I could eat what and when I wanted.

Enter my daughter, Sarah, eight or so years later.

There is a Beethoven concert at her church outside Cincinnati, for which they lack a suitable baritone, and she would be "over the moon" if I did it with them. Another call informs me that Janet, her mother, says she will break my legs if I don't do it. Yet a third entreaty details reasons why it would be a great memory for Sarah to sing with me, since—did I say?—she will be doing the alto solos.

Sarah then goes into the hospital for ankle surgery. When I call to ask how she is, her husband says the boys, my grandsons, would be so excited too. I say I haven't heard that little piece of leverage. The response is that Sarah has been waiting to employ it only if needed, that and calling Arlene to assist in the twisting. Wanting to have her wake from the operation to good news, I pass some along: I will do the concert.

While it is true that I have seldom heard Sarah sound so happy, it is just as true that all my nocturnal neuroses have never been happier with a parking place: every time I talk, I feel my voice. Every time I go out at night, I think how I am tiring that organ. Every time I eat during the day, I wonder how much phlegm it is going to give me, to say nothing of the potential for reflux, since the surgery doesn't always hold, or take care of the psychosomatic aspects of the condition that one has been living with for fifty-plus years. Being a supposed type of athlete, I now have to wonder about everything I do in relation to my general health. I even have to watch my alcohol consumption. How will I self-nourish?

Life as a non-singer had been good, now that I had one. For that main reason, I never gave my voice a legitimate try after the surgery. On occasion, I would let fly a few tones, either in a lesson, or on my own. Invariably it "sucked" and to the extent that I would note again how glorious it was not to have to worry about it.

Arlene, too, would let slip how much she missed the sound of my voice, also making music together. Sometimes I would even think, gee, wouldn't it be fun to take part in this concert or that, or, temporarily wasting a semester's-worth of longevity on the faculty of some school, look through rose-colored glasses at the recitals I used to give. Through it all, I had the advantage of knowing that if I took a deep breath and counted to ten, such impulses would vaporize.

"Fie-ing" on myself for having said yes to my daughter, I started sticking my big toe into the vocal deep end, knowing I would have to do so to even perform "Come to Jesus" in whole notes without cracking. The first day was awful, as were the second and third. For the fourth I was actually able to stand myself in a few middle-voiced exercises, but generally found it to be drudgery, accompanied by a prayer: "Get thee hence, Satan and Thank you, God, that I am no longer a singer. Get me through just one more torturous round, and I won't trouble You on the subject again."

But, the Deity sat in the other team's dugout. Little by little, it was, that the bass-baritone started to feel, instead of old, like that *of* old; no, better. I would go into my former library when in Kentucky, where sat the piano I sold the new owners, and sing in those live acoustics. I began to get "The Feeling," the inclination to do it, in my throat. In spite of myself, I started to muse on situations in which I could even get paid for it again and, before long, was panicking that no one would want me anymore. Thanks to the surgery, I would not be having to worry about staying "vocalized up," or getting sick before performances.

Arlene and I are committed to a cruise to the Bahamas for her mother's 80th birthday. Before we leave, I get laryngitis and can't stay in vocal shape for any of the trip in the car, or where we stayed for several days in North Carolina, maybe even the trip back at the expense of Arlene's ears.

I "am" once again my résumé, miserable and paranoid, since laryngitis doesn't last that long and something more serious must be wrong. I call my doctor, wait through the agony of some crap while on hold, only to be told I had to call back on the very day I hit the shores and can't get a referral to the ENT till I see head honcho PCP- barely older than my grandson, Danny.

I hate singing all over, moreover the medical community. Lo and behold, though, my voice starts coming around, now that I am back in war zones. A woman from Germany staying in our apartment is floored by my vocalizing, and I am not even well yet.

Where was that résumé, anyway? I should read it. Just think! If I could tap my old sources and break back in, imagine how gratifying it would be, sounding like this at my age. And say, could I not get that part of my persona back, do something artistic along with all the property purchases, mix them together and be the complete man I always wanted, though with a *real* job.

My old teacher said Met tenor Richard Tucker used to do fur-trader deals on the payphone between acts. Isn't that really the idea? Singing, really all of art, should be a natural part of your life. Isn't it even supposed to imitate it, or some such? You know, I eat, I sleep, I make love, therefore I make music! How great is that? I never realized the young *singing* life is wasted on the young too!! I'm starting to feel like the person my materials say I am.

Pardon me just a minute. // // Ahem.

I'll wind this up later. That damned nasal spray my teenage doctor gave me is kind of drying my throat out. Why did I take it anyway? He had to ask me what I meant by "high notes," describing my symptoms. Jesus!! Not sure it helps the phlegm either. I'd best go in, chug some water; maybe even do the sinus douche. Don't know when the woman from Berlin is coming back home. Now that she thinks I'm good, I don't want to give her the impression it's a student in the studio instead of me. I'll just warm it up a little again now, you know, see-if-it-is-still-there kind of thing.

Oh, Lord!! I've been around so many people with colds lately. One was in the elevator this morning. Ugh. You know, there is a fine line between a dry palate and the beginning of a real sore throat. Hmmm. Ahem. La, la, la. "Vee-oh-vah-vee." Let's see, when is my student getting here? I'd best get this over before... before.... Excuse me.

*

I think that stuff I had for lunch gave me some gunk too. And that damned pollen better be out of southern Ohio before get there. Plus, I am staying with Paul and he smokes. I'd best sleep over at my former house, beginning several nights before the concert; of course, there is all that mildew over there...... you know, I really think my throat *may* be getting sore.....ahem.

*

Vocalizing wasn't too bad. Still not totally right since the laryngitis, but… I wanted to get all the stuff out before my student gets here. Teaching always puts an extra demand on your voice, and now that I'm doing some demonstration during the lessons again, it does so doubly. Think writing makes me dry too, sitting here in one position, you know? Maybe I should go lie down before my student arrives. I wish he'd cancel……..

Twenty-To-Life In A Phone Cell

Monday:

You know all the things a mind can do.

Breakfasting with a friend yesterday, I mentioned the university where I once taught. It didn't so much as cross my mind the rest of the day, but last night what do I do? Dream about it; that I was back there, wrestling with the divas and devils. It was a nightmare.

You've noticed, too, how in dreams things look completely different, yet you understand perfectly who and what they are? The university was that way, unlike anything I ever actually saw there. My hulking colleagues, one Mastodon in particular, were shriveled; the skinny-lipped Goebbels types, puffy and elephantine. Yet there was no question of recognizing them, from, if nothing else, the "Gaudeamus Icki-Tour"* feeling in the pit of my stomach.

*Pun on the old Latin student song," Gaudeamus Igitur." Quoted in certain pieces of classical music, most notably the   Brahms Academic Festival Overture.

The experience set me to thinking: nightmares, daily life, *au courant* values. If one dreams about what occupies his mind during waking hours, I'm in some deep doo-doo. My skirmishes with the cell phone armies have escalated to a major campaign.

There's this song from one of the Gian Carlo Menotti operas, in which a person in some totalitarian society screams, "Papers, papers, papers" to the point of insanity. For me it is "Phones, phones, everywhere phones."

I read about a bank robber the other day that chatted somebody up on her phone while pointing the gun. A good half of the (gazillion) people I see sitting at New York City sidewalk cafés—whether in someone's company or not—are talking on their phones. Who are they talking to? Easy: the people yelling into their own contraptions meeting me as I walk on down. I'm not bothered we have the bloody things, see, so much that they're security blankets.

You pull up to a jetway in an airplane; by the time the overhead lights are on, two thirds of the passengers have whipped out their phones, booted up and pasted them to their ears; worse still, their mouths. Mothers in diners sit there while their kids act like renegades as they catch up on their phone time. There was an old Twilight Zone-type show I saw once that has haunted me for years. A guy goes to sleep, only to dream of being caught in some evil society installed in the house next door. Each night they get their claws into him a little more, before sending him back. His dream eventually becomes reality, and he never returns.

I know, I know. I'm personifying that old Biblical prophecy, "That which I feared most is come upon me." But I can't help it. I'm building up to my own nightmare of the house next door, only with people driving me berserk squawking on their phones. What hell!

Me, I don't take my phone with me half the time anymore; don't want to be one of *them* having someone think I can't cut the umbilical cord. I feel that way even though I'll never see any of the people looking at me again. It's like when I eat in the car: I hold the sandwich down low when someone passes, so he/she won't think I would contribute to such decadence.

On the rare occasions I pull mine out in public (the phone, I mean), usually because it's vibrating in my pants. I don't really talk to anyone; don't need to. I wait for the "message completed" buzz and listen. But walking on by, just listening and not disturbing anyone, I realize that to the hoards I am one OF them. They've no thought that this is rare for me; that I don't normally bellyache through the ethers at the street level. I want to run up to each person, shaking him, crying that I don't further his delinquencies, minor or major. The only time I really need my phone anyway is driving cross-country, where three-fourths of the trip it doesn't work anyway, there being too few church steeples left in the world for the transmitter towers.

I'm thinking of making this big statement, you understand, like people used to with their credit cards or their bras: burning them or turning them back to the company, even paying a cancellation fee. I sold my farm anyway and won't be driving that much. I might even wear a blown-up ATT "cancelled" bill around my neck. It wouldn't be as loony as half the things Lady Gaga or Miley Cyrus do.

Arlene once got a new, super fancy model. It (and she) were so jacked-up that half the time it wouldn't call anybody anyway, even places where there *are* church steeples. It caused her (and me) more consternation than having to use payphones. What sense does that make? I at least assumed I'd be able to reach her then. No geek she, though, which I also love her for, she forgets to turn the ringer on a good half the time and just doesn't bother to answer the other half. I think the sound it makes is a mystery to her, like the old farmer who took his new chainsaw back to the store, complaining he could only get it to cut one cord of wood instead of the advertised three. When the clerk pulled the started cord, the farmer exclaimed, "What's that noise?"

I wouldn't let on to Arlene, but at times I actually think her phone is pretty cool, especially that one time I got through. It can do about anything except sweep out, once she remembers to hang up: it's a phone, email, database, camera, music player, internet connection, and one other thing I can't remember, all in one: oh, a coin-operated washer I think it was.

There was this guy in my New York apartment building. He had a condition—you know, whacked and brilliant all at once. Days-long obsessions would overtake him, which he would sometimes hurl at me mid-sidewalk and mid-sentence: "These people on drugs! It's TAIRRIBLE," or hours later and blocks away, "THESE GODDAMNED DRUGS! IT'S TAIRRIBLE!" And, "AIR

CONDITIONING! IT'S A SHAME. JUST GET A FAN," he would say, waving his hand, rattling off every baseball player's birthday. He knew the day of my birth before I met him. My Swedish wife should have consulted him; seven years together and she couldn't remember mine.

Anyway, this guy and I were in the elevator one day and hadn't even said hello for four floors. Just before he stepped out, he (apparently) added, "No, the sister was more compassionate. But she's gone to Peru!"

The way this guy was, see, is how I fear getting to be with cell phones. You see me out on Broadway, it's not, "Hey, Happy New Year; how you doin'?" But, "….these goddamned cell phone FREAKAZOIDS! It's a frickin' NIGHTMARE. Jesus, Maria, Josef!"

Remember that quite un-PC story about a certain national group of scientists who train a frog to jump on command and want to see how the training held up under pain? Upon severing the fourth leg and the frog didn't jump, they concluded that, subjected to too much pain, the frog went deaf.

Cell-Phonies are just like that: they don't get the much-publicized brain cancer, they're just brain *dead*! The minute someone whips out his phone, let alone uses it, he's deaf, dumb, blind, loses his balance, and every scrap of manners his mother taught him.

Arlene and I were walking out of a yogurt shop the other night. Some clown is bouncing up the street, yakking his head off, oblivious. He not only makes it impossible for us to have a conversation, but runs smack into me, and then slams the door in Arlene's face. Worse still, it doesn't even register with him. It's not just what people do—which in a way you can understand—on their phones, so much as being too out of it to realize anything afterward.

A woman and her daughter were—considerately, actually—chatting in muted tones behind me in a grocery store line when, out of the otherwise checkout blue, the older one bams: **"MOM? WE'RE AT GRISTEDES! THE GROCERY STORE......'G-R-I-S-T-E—**

'…... ANYTHING YOU WANT ME TO GET YOU?…. NO, MY CELL …. IT'S A TELEPHONE….. YOU SURE?….OKAY….SEE YOU IN A BIT."

She turns around, apologizes for bashing me with her cart before the phone rang, but says nothing about sending me to my ENT for eardrum replacement.

Then this moron at the vegetable mart last Sunday testing the avocados startles me with, "HMM, SOFT AND JUICY"! Happy to find a guacamole-able one myself, what with the playoff game starting in two hours, I say, "Ripe, eh?" When he didn't respond, I glance over and see the earphones. He's not even talking to me or about the avocados OR the game. He stands there, I don't know how long, vicariously squeezing every goddamned Haas avocado ten times and never sees me. At least I knew my deodorant held.

And phones are noise polluters, you know? You're alone in the park, enjoying perfect serenity: suddenly you get, **"...And she didn't even apologize!!"** from around the rocks Central Park boulders. Plus I'm sick of assuming someone is addressing me when they're shouting into one of those mother-freaking headsets. I don't think I'll ever get used to it, and of course, the guy wearing it always gives you this "trying-not-to-act-like-I-think-you-are-a-complete-moron-by-concluding-for-even-an-instant-in-this-day-and-age-that-I-would-actually-be-talking-to-*you*" look.

They tell me phones are now being replaced by this little watch-like gizmo you wear on your arm or elsewhere. I guess they have blow-up TV screens or some such in them. They should link well up with grocery store checkout monitors I'm hearing about. I can hardly wait; I need a break: someone raising an arm and screaming into his wrist for a change. I can see it now, though: for ten years I'll probably think they're about to slug me.

I already feel belligerent by these considerate darlings that involve me in their private lives, holding speaker phones two feet out in front of them on the bus. I'll get with it soon, though, because they have a wonderful built-in advantage: you get both parties' points of view. I do hate feeling left out.

To my own reader, though, be true: I'm not as third-worldly as I seem, even though my students scold me for being so "retro," grabbing java at Pain Quotidien. I realize, for instance, cell phones have educational value. Before my breakfast hangout closed, I took note of the phone brands that fade in and out. Sitting there munching my Eggs Florentine, trying to mind my own business, I'd hear their owners screaming all the way to the east side. You can't afford to have a phone like that. I think it was a Motorola. I noticed their stock tanked about that time; must be why. Such knowledge does, for instance, come in handy around Christmas, learning (vicariously, of course) the gifting brands to stay away from. *Do you hear what I hear?*

Oh, and Philadelphia isn't atmospherically conducive. Had you noticed? Something around the Schuylkill* is a Signal-kill. Mid-bagel

*The river that runs through Philadelphia.

some gal the other day nailed me with, "YOU'RE IN PHILADELPHIA?!," all the way to Rittenhouse Square, clearly with the naked voice through the ethers. With lungs like that, why waste money on an iOS?

Perhaps my favorite diner experience was when the restaurant's house phone *and* the owner's cell went off at about the same time. He would walk around talking with one on each ear. I mean it wasn't Wall Street, for Christ sake!

Oh, and the Stroller Chauffeurs! Always dangerous, but when Babbling Bertha pops up pushing a "dualy" beating her gums on an Android, it's Lethal Weapon VI!

I know I should rethink. Robert's Rules of Society usually doesn't hesitate to tell me I am the one out of order. Two phones may be necessary in today's world. I do in fact see more and more people armed with "multis." After all, do we not have two ears?

I sat next to one such young man in the doctor's office the other day: he had three of them. An amiable young four-hundred-pounder he was, and ....

Oh, damn. I gotta get off all this sh...

*

Friday morning, 3:11 am

I'm exhausted; haven't slept since Sunday when I had that colleague dream. I'm terrified, afraid to nod off; think I'm gonna have the cellular version. Hassled as I am, I still .. .don'.... wanna....di .....whoa ..

Friday afternoon, T-Mobil, Midtown:

I passed out in the wee hours, unable to fight it any longer. Sure enough, there I was standing in front of some shit-hook in a black robe, about to be sentenced. I didn't even know what for. His body, a black rectangle, glass pasted across what face he had. He wore these goggles that read "I-Pad, You-Pad, We all Pad!" Standing two feet from him, the schmuck had the gall to call me on my phone to deliver the sentence: twenty-to-life. I fainted.

As in any other dream, when I came to I knew where I was: **The Village of the Phone-Damned:** smelly, disgusting room with vertical bars, people in the recesses making sub-glottal noises like the Montreal Symphony playing Murray Schaffer, only into their phones. It was Hi-Tech Dickens: gibberish starting soft, then building with intermittent honk-like outbursts—in cockney no less—to things like:

"GAWD!!!….. **….GAWD,** YEAH, PICK UP, WILL YOU?"

Other semi-human clusters, just hanging, letting their phones ring and ring, then ring some more, the way they do in cafes when customers around you really wanna piss you off: screening their calls, rings set at "17," the volume on "Wake the Dead."

But, *these* guys, they just stared at me and smiled, vacantly; toothless, eyes like donuts. Ecstasyville. Metharama. I began to make out creatures as my eyes adjusted: grotesque bunches of ears on the same head, looking like boiled *"Ris de Veau."* The real torture was that EACH ear had a Treo with wand like Arlene's old one, plastered to it, their mouths working loud and fast, enough to cover every conversation at once, as if they had more than one mouth too. Pure agony.

Now *I* was crying "GAWD!" I was in cell phone hell!

Then like a grand finale, I look up to see this semi coming at me! An eighteen-wheel baby stroller, steam rolling out of the darkness, smoke belching from upright mufflers: images of nude women with pirate lettering across: **"BIG WIRELESS BERTHA. LOOK OUT, HONEY"** ...... driven by this rouge-cheeked Virago, standing atop the cab with a set of reins, a whip cracking and hissing in the dank, getting closer and closer and closer to me, when.....!!!! Dingalingaling!!!

* *

I guess it was like they say about dreams in which you're falling: if you hit bottom before you wake up, you die. Some idiot on the other end wanted to know if Alison was there.

Then I remembered: blacking out, I'd dropped my phone. The last thing I did was call to get my service terminated, ironically leaving it on. It rang just when "Big Wireless Bertha" was about to flatten me. Every person in The Village of the Phone-Damned vaporized; I woke.

My first reaction was, "GAWD!..... Thank you for my cell phone." I hate to think what would have happened if it hadn't rung. I may have even kissed it, offered one of my own up to the Deity. With nothing to wake me, I would have been imprisoned, permanently; maybe dead.

First thing I did this morning was reinstate my service. And I know what I'll do tonight too: take an Ambien. Addiction-schmichten. They're "lights out" and you don't dream as much on them.

Thank God I'm a 21st Century kind 'a guy.

That Rotten Something In The State Of Opera

Dateline/Opera@duh/duh/duh.or.tank

It is as simple as this: people who do not appreciate the emotional power of the human voice reproducing works of the great masters should move on to less rarefied air.

The art form known as opera in particular exists on a separate plane from what such cliff dwellers are ever likely to understand, and for them I feel truly sorry. Many of them working as opera professionals are transplants from musical theater (formerly known as Broadway), and spoken drama. When it comes to them, I feel sorry for the rest of us.

To wit: In classical music, if you sing, you act and can't avoid it. If you sing well, you act well; if you sing poorly, you act poorly; you cannot separate the two realms.

Unfortunately for opera, we have lost sight of those precepts, choosing to see acting as something one tacks on. When Robert Merrill was kicked out the Met for a year or so for making a movie, he went to see a performance at the MET wherein he first heard Mario Del Monaco and was flabbergasted. My friend Michael heard Franco Corelli for the first time in the 1960s and had a similar reaction. You opera-lovers: do you think their being so moved had anything to do with the way these singers "acted"?

If you sing well in opera, but do something that looks awkward, you don't act (communicate) well, much worse in fact than if you just stood there. Conversely, if you do something that looks good but don't sing well, you act much worse in that particular genre, no matter how good you look. True, one can make certain motions and sounds that get across basic ideas without disturbing the real intent. "Basic," however, being the operative word, anything that attempts to go beyond it may succeed in other art forms, but does not in opera.

Expand your definition of singing technique to include not only producing pearl-shaped tones, with accurately-sung, simple emotional expression, and you are half way there. As an Upper West Side butcher once told Arlene, "Get the best ingredients and don't fuck it up."

If you have read me previously, you know what a geezer I am. This chapter's geezerliness had its origins long before the current Age of Opera Insult. Being behind, or ahead, of the world in the 1970s, I would note in disgust a TV "Celebrity Roast," shown on one channel at the same time as a "Live at Lincoln Center" presentation of opera on the other, the Roast's having the same flavor as the intermission features of the (opera) telecast, and to many people's certain delight.

I have always thought something known as classical should be held to a higher standard. Art in general should have nothing to do with entertainment, marketing, or, in its purest form, box office. Today, PBS channels solve the problem more easily than they once did. Reserved for what had little or no means of support other than speaking (singing) for itself, it is now a fund drive contaminated with indiscriminate products and has been a major fusion of the confusion, and no fountain into which I will be seen tossing my coins.

Take a look at current editions of opera magazines. They are like others you see on the newsstands: designed for the commercial, for the people who have no inkling as to the contradiction between art and entertainment. If for no other reason, art should be above entrepreneurial mastication because it is one of the few remaining ways to tell the difference in the two.

Remove the glamour, and you take the first step toward restoring opera to an approach in which visual attitudes are merely suggested, with the music supplying anything else that could possibly be needed. Let singers be faithful to, not only their scores, but the lessons taught them by their faded mentors. Then we will have performances that, unless you are approaching old age, you have never witnessed. It was called the Golden Age of Opera.

Yet the underlying premise of this chapter relates to why concert versions of opera are often more successful than staged ones. Why? More than any other single reason, opera requires the element of listener imagination, the state of being completely transported and transcended. Infuse it with attempts at commingled realism, and you jolt your listener wide awake, back into the realm of Nightly News. It is art on two levels and does not succeed anymore than a war on two fronts.

Today we place great emphasis on what should be little more than ancillary components. But too many people paying today's prices for tickets don't know that, don't know they are making it an elitist art form, and simply assume it is better the way they have been conditioned. Worse still, the opera professionals of the world are failing them as to their education. Half the time they leave the theater pissed off and don't know why.

Though one does hear good singing in certain venues, all in all the art form continues on its downward spiral, not only for the level of performance and opera company, but for a performer's career as well: too few last long. The physical requirements of microphone-less intensive phonating dictate that the majority of mental concentration be on the production of their voices, and that there be much time to both train and rest afterward, much like that of a baseball starting pitcher's arm.

The world and what it demands has changed, but the human body not. One illustration of it I remember from my student days was opera expert Tony Randall, speaking on the (Texaco) MET Opera Quiz, lamenting the fact that, though a singer of sorts himself, he could not physically get through one opera aria. When I was a student, such things were taken for granted; now we have lost sight of them.

In addition to my main teacher, it was from a stage director that I first awakened to these concepts, in specific his describing what a wonderful *dramatic* experience he had been given watching Jussi Björling stand perfectly still onstage, but singing in a way that really moved him. That stage director was one of what nowadays they almost never are: a musician. He is also now old enough to likely be either retired, or even deceased.

The formula for operatic credibility stands in opposition to what the modern age has tried but failed to achieve it by: unspoiled singing— therefore drama—that will stand on its own. It works without trappings. Witness the countless productions in the city of New York alone that, leaving you stone cold, despite all the stage machinery of a returning Jedi. If the approach to today's opera with all its costs did the trick, one could at least present a cogent argument. As it is, they pile the operatic killing fields higher and higher.

Omit the diva perfume lines, the brands of clothing, the phony head (and tit) shots, the Hollywood-esque "star" interviews, and replace them with study, rest, physical and mental preparation, and you will take the first steps toward the return of opera as staged music. As

Arturo Toscanini once said to a well-known singer, "The stars are in the sky." Another podium great, Fritz Reiner, eventually left the Met over his insistence that the choristers, even in "Die Fledermaus," not be expected to sing lying down.

The best and longest-enduring classical singers have usually been rather plain, home-body types that preserve themselves for their art, as opposed to catering to the tiring and physically drying-out activities like photo shoots, appearing too much in public, talking, and almost anything else that involves looking any way that is not relaxing and natural. As Leontyne Price (who should know) once said, "A rested body is a rested voice." I would take it a step further: a rested voice *requires* a rested body. One sees her at events now that she is retired; previously, not much.

I know people that have spent their entire adult lives involved with opera, but who (now) say they don't even like the art form. I so do not wonder why. Something drastic may have to become the artistic equivalent of planetary life after a super volcano, or a nuclear explosion to right the ship. It could be in principle from the same hand as the preservation of architectural specimens: poverty, the best friend an old structure ever had, and doubtfully chosen on purpose.

By the same token that I personally doubt God lays much store by kneeling on benches and prayer rugs, wearing yarmulkes, dunking ourselves in water and crossing ourselves, I believe that Giuseppe Verdi knew how benefit of what he had created was to me achieved, and was little interested in elements beyond beautifully reproducing what he wrote; or that of Wagner, who wanted best singers, usually Italians of the period, unlike what we think of as "Wagnerian" today. In the heyday of Musical Theater, even Richard Rogers demanded fidelity to his scores. *Great composers take care of the rest.*

The least severe critique my words herein will earn me is, "Old School." As I see it, we live in a world that is too much governed, not by how something is, but by how it looks anyway; too attentive to form, not content. Attend a board meeting of an arts organization; the first and last word is likely to be how a project is marketed, most likely in the location and image of daily palisades. I am here to say that, even in a capitalist society, the right artistic product doesn't need much marketing, and that if it does, something about it is already rotten.

What was called the Golden Age of Opera was that in which singers basically looked elegant, even if obese, stood and sang their hearts out, carrying the audience along with them in a state of client-building, semi-conscious bliss. But such an approach requires accurate, *technically* good, and unmolested re-creations of the masterworks, which depend on rehearsals specifically devoted to that end, then reproduced on the stage.

The further we depart from "All the Gold" of that age,* the closer we approach the different world of Musical Theater (formerly known as "Broadway"), and the more downhill momentum we accrue with its vastly different requirements. As one of my best professors said to a class of us youngsters, "In all things, direct your singing to the one person in the audience who knows the difference."

The vortex of the gathering information in this chapter's message is illustrated by the success of radio and recorded music, or the reading a play versus seeing it in its finite version onstage. The imagin-

---

*"All that Gold" is the name of an aria from the Menotti's opera, Amahl and the Night Visitors.

ation has no possible rival and must dominate all considerations for classical art forms to be truly successful. Some great literary minds have called it, "The willing suspension of disbelief."

Not that we read so much anymore, taking in what we get passively. If we do read, my impression is we do so with scant reference to the classics. Remember the last time you read a piece of literature? Being involved in something elegant from the past likely changes the way you think, feel, and even speak, and most definitely for the better. And it all achieved through the unparalleled workings of the mind!

Cessation of the above pejorative habits represents half the journey. Then, in place of cartoon characters flopping through hoops and trashing their voices, one must in turn utilize the freed-up time well: coach and rehearse, coach and rehearse, coach and rehearse the singers offstage before they are hoisted onto it.

Opera does indeed represent a fusion of the arts. But the more we fuse it with *other* arts, moreover, allow them to gain prominence, the more the Muse faintly fades from view. The Muse's function is to lift listeners one out of their daily humdrum, not bring them down to it. No opera dog wagged by his tail will accomplish it or long endure, anymore than one (dog) that chases cars.

There was that story of a man standing on his rooftop, eying encroaching floodwaters. As a boat, then a helicopter come by to rescue him, he rejects each, answering, "Go on. Go on. God will save me." Eventually he drowns and arrives at the throne of God, whereupon he asks about it, to which God replies, "I don't know what happened; I sent you a boat and a helicopter."

The word is out, the floating and twirling vessels dispatched. Yet, I fear we will merrily fuse and amuse ourselves along the way, artistic noses just above water, past the long-awaited hydroplane swooping in for the rescue. All earth—and heavenly—bound fuels for *transportation* will yet be buried beneath the shale: crude, unrefined, and otherwise out of gas.

Retort To "Retort"

DH Lawrence, not especially known for his poetry, nevertheless wrote some good ones. Perhaps the most famous is the "Rocking Chair Boy." Another that always stuck out in my mind is, I assume, also the shortest one. It's called *Retort to Jesus*. That two line poem says something to the effect that anyone who forces himself to love someone he doesn't really love, and commits a "murder in his own heart."

I have my own version.

Because, and correctly so, I am run out of "Dodge" by rules of society which forbid to me hate or otherwise discriminate against any human being for reasons of race religion, or sexual orientation, then neither should I be forced TO love anyone for the same reasons, lest I commit a murder in *my* own heart.

I long for an epoch in which people can make decisions based on people as people, not specimens of a certain identification, origination, and membership, or what may have happened in different eras to different people by different hand-wielders with different needs.

I even think parades honoring different races, orientations, and national origins are divisive.

But the time for that kind of thing to me looks, as yet, far off, just as my own personal one draws ever nigh.....

Beneath The Doric Columnist

Obviously progressing to a more unhinged state as the book comes near its ending, the idea for this little vignette was to put something down that bore not one trace of inspiration, or even form. I'm good that sort of thing, I know, and have been doing it all along, you say. Thanks.

> My Barnes and Noble sojourns do daily carry on:
> Through mud, though snow,
> When Arlene's in the studio,
> Hoping to get me a little 'booky." You know?

In pedestrian flight, things come to me. I fear this is the ghost of inspiration present, but hold fast against the tide. Here is one such *viene-a-moi* tidbit: good writing is the most stuff-demanding thing a person can do. Amongst the big everything, it can be almost anything, if at least two-pronged, though in most publishing houses, your prong, for once, would seldom get you squat.

Having something to say though, might, even stringing things together in a halfway intelligible manner could also. But that too could, in the words of our former lord the pope relative to other religions, be insufficient, there being only so many cow paths around Robin Hood's barn, or of offering up a hearty "Merry Christmas" on a cold winter's night.

Take my oldest grandson, who one Yuletide—that of only his sixth year—to Arlene asserted, "Uncle Alex is quite the builder." The grandson could be a writer, but only if even he has something *about* which to write.

One isn't really advised to wander about organizing pretty words, calling it a career, despite examples that lie desultorily about the first floor of said destination of daily sojourns. Combining something to say and something well said with what is nowadays is called your "platform," submitted, fingers fully crossed, to your favorite publishing house Jennifer and, whoopee, you might keep off the leaning tower of query rejects. But that method too might be another ghost of Christmas, in this case, Past.

All things considered, this writing thing really does take quite the person as well as the builder. Why then so many fully published writers are so fully ignoble, or why what they produce brings out such full frontal ignobility, I haven't quite the clue. But, quite clearly, I should write about *that*. Could this, then, be the inspiration I so won't suffer?

No wonder historians are scribes. They have brains where singers have pretty sounding noise makers, they or couldn't get their facts straight, those and all those historian-words: "seminal," "phaeton," "vertiginous," "rock-ribbed," that they may or may not have real knowledge concerning. Second, being mostly professors in order to not quite starve, they'd never get promoted without drawing some written attention. Thirdly, they have great benefit packages, including graduate assistants to do their grunt work, leaving time for the advancing carpal tunnel, as well as medical coverage to treat it. *Voilà* (or as I constantly hear, "oila"*) again, and Hats Off, Gentlemen, a Genius.*

With all the smarts, for instance, "a"** Shelby Foote possessed, he additionally had the good sense to call himself "writer," rather than historian. With all his knowledge, I'm not sure where that leaves the

---

* Refers to Critic Hanslick in the times of Brahms, who said, "Hats of, gentlemen, a genius." The fictitious PDQ Bach character created by comedian Peter Schickile, supposedly discovering the music of PDQ in a garage can, saying, "Hats back on, gentlemen, an idiot."

** Sports lingo

rest of the writing world; unable to say what it has little real knowledge of, I would guess.

Since much of the learning *and* writing I encounter amounts to digging up old bones to put in new graves, (you rang, academia?), I like doing it (writing, I mean) based simply on what I think. About the worst that can be said (instead of "sued") of me is that someone didn't care for my conclusions, though had a concrete notion of what I wanted to say. To my surprise, by the way, I find I am not lacking in that realm. Check your hands; I dare say there is a sizeable distance between them.

One cannot effectively nay-say an opinion, assuming one is stated, following, even, an appearance on "The View," "Hardball," or "Hannity." At least so I nightly pray in the wee radio hours to the accompaniment of John Batchelor, George Nori and, formerly, Art Bell.

But here lies the inspiration-less rub: a mere hybrid it nevertheless leaves me. I can scarcely avoid being the product of what others exhale, yea though I walk through the valley of only one plowed-through short-story or the feared-evil of a solitary conversation: thou art with me and I am, yea, not discernible from the masses of massed humanity drilling my gonads on the way to breakfast, and would have had to be brought up by Sashquatch to be otherwise.

I could have called this, my formless-est and least inspired chapter, "Beneath The *Dork* Columnist" too, much like that piece I wrote lo those many years ago, and even before I read that piece of Dave Barry's, referring to "Hoppalong Dork." But that piece on mine, written on my Sabbatical on my back porch was just plain daffy, as opposed to the bare half-assed—or half bare-assed—way I often write now, not even half-bearingly the now me. Nevertheless, when I ran across its dogged ears plugging up a mouse hole in the corner of my hall closet—formerly occupied by pictures of Arlene in various snapshots with old boyfriends—pause, or, I guess, pose, to ask what was duly tendered: just what, pray tell, and *who* is underneath a writer's layers that gives rise to the bare-assedest of impulses?

Why, for instance, tying my shoes most mornings do I think of my father, except that my sunken arches have to this day never felt so good as when he bound them up for the concrete-est of reasons, specifically that I had not at yet acquired the motor skill to do it; but why would I have even a half-laced, half-shod, *or the* half-assed-est of inclinations to put such a thing on paper? My brother-in-law would say it was quite the silliness, only without the "quite." Could this obsession, then, be senility in the absence of inspiration I so don't desire?

There are—*of course*—as many types of writing as there are writers; rather, more, when you consider those who moonlight under pseudonyms, as well as their real *nyms*. Their publishers, of course, still get first nyms. If a tree falls in the forest, is the husband still wrong and the writer poor?

My Swedish girlfriend—the one couldn't remember the date of my birth—normally confused all that forest stuff. I was, naturally, always wrong, but from time to time she'd come up with confused, therefore entertaining, verbal blends of my best *pro forma* one liners: "Does a bear shit in the woods" and "Is the Pope a Catholic?" would become, "Does thee pope shit in thee woods." Only in the early days, traipsing through the Polish woods I would hazard re that particular pope.

Damned, if I don't appear to be succumbing to inspiration over this pope thing! I'll save it, though. Maybe close out the whole enterprise with something on spiritual higher-ups, something perhaps re their exit strategies: you know, "Old Popes Never Die, Just Fade From..." I'm a little concerned it will offend some really good Catholics though, especially those who don't know how my mind works. Perhaps I'll make it a totally fictitious one-act, sketching the first real encounter with the Deity, asking at the conclusion of the one and only real audience with the one and only real Holy Father to please stand. Prithee, lest this nonsense should fall into the hands of Danish cartoonists, carry across for the next lofty and, in that case, *inspired* installment. And do know above all that I really do love Catholics, many of whom are my best friends...

But back to the absence of same, the current piece could be almost anything and still quite the justified one, especially with no implied history (mine) as a writer. Since at one time I thought of naming it either the "Final Roundup" (also known as a weed killer) or "Peter Piper Bitched Back some Pickled Peppers" (also known as a fairy tale), a list of unadorned gripes holds greatest sway for realizing the first paragraph parameters.

For if I should set down something of my life as a columnist, it would have to be like Tricky Dick and Rosemary's* eighteen famous minutes: silence, in this case, a blank piece of paper, not that I'd be able to convey it on whatever has replaced the typesetter.

Previously noted, being the columnist I wasn't gave me the experience I wouldn't, that is in academia, have: enthusiasm! Or was it hope? For I felt a hint of what it must be like to be someone with a real life, instead of one merely unraveling his—or *with* his—God-given talent, such as a singer. Any large-footed forest recluse knows singers aren't people, that very thing being what I taught the readers of my non-columns. And, was it not a beautiful thing? Since my Kentucky neighbors knew me as "The Educated Guy," was I not already frontrunner for head freak of the county anyway? "What, he writes too?"

Returning with me now from those thrilling days of yesteryear, just who is it that I am? Have I covered it, given thee the right reasons,

---

*President Nixon and assistant Rosemary who are believed to erased eighteen minutes of tape, relevant to the Watergate scandal

who—or what—ever shits in the woods? Do you know me? I wouldn't want to turn in an incomplete set of essays on the merely skimmed-over subject of me.

Forest denizen or not, I once read a piece I liked by Joseph Epstein called, *In a Snob-Free Zone.* He winds up trying to illustrate the snob he thinks he is, but, to me, fails. He's a nice guy. What does that say of me? I am more of a snob the he. Were it not so, I would have said, "him." But now let's focus, or as I constantly hear, "Focus in:" I am an irascible thing and bitch well nigh constantly, always have, always will. Arlene says I am getting worse too, even since moving to North Carolina, or as they say in rural Kentucky, "worser." I can be a real *son*-of-a-bitch too. My daughter tells me my second grandson takes after me because he has a temper, well, coupled with a few other things. But that kind of thing (or *"a"* thing, as I also hear all over the place) is something I own; something that provides my very own paper trail, my being not yet dead, certainly not yet dug up and trotted over to another grave. My origins are proudly my own.

Things just piss me off, see? Like walking the streets of New York. No one EVER moves over. Where is the give, the 50-50? And the sub-humans, those weekend parents and nanny-parents, who haven't the sense to realize the child-wheelies they sling around like Hiaigh-Liaghi sticks, stick out four feet in front of them, not where their own upright bodies are. Why don't they wake up earlier of a weekend morning to be parents, crowding the diners where I have my very own *Stamm-Tisch* ?*

And why do all these nut jobs have to scream at each other all the time when essentially *conversing?* Especially the school beasts: I know they have all that pent up energy, and that being made to act halfway civilized for a few hours is a strain. But, Jesus, can't they let off steam in a way that doesn't send me into shock? Of course, as my friend Reshma would say, I am musician, my ears sensitive:

> I cup them when subway-faced,
> React to sudden noises braced,
> That other people don't notice a trace:

1) City motor vehicle operators, for instance. The typical New York driver blasts first, thinks second, if at all. And why always absolutely "<u>lay</u>" on the horn? What about a little "peck" for your purposes? To a pedestrian like me, it is grotesquely jolting.

---

* German for a permanently-reserved, "standing" table.

2) Loudspeakers in an airplane or on the subway–even the door closing tones–maxed out. 3) And why can't people learn to talk? My sister's husband—my brother-in-law, the same—can't resist taking shots at me. I went to college and he didn't so he has to try to make me look bad, especially in front of other family members. But that mental defective says, "ideal" for "idea," plus a bunch of other ignorant things. 4) And where did all our current, half-baked language trends come from? English has a "U" vowel, in which case, except when coming after an "r," a "y" sound in front is correct, or at least acceptable before the "oo" part. But that doesn't include words spelled in most other ways. I constantly hear "tyoo" for "two" and "nyoon" for "noon," and "dyoo" for "do." Even the professional speaker over the CVS pharmacy automated line says "tyoo." But, then you already know about my gripes with so-called talking professionals.

One of my best students has that "yoo" thing going on her outgoing cell phone message, and her mother is a copulating English teacher! What is the world coming tyoo? 5) And what William Saffire called, "Up talk": the lingo of the teeny-bopper, going vocally up at the end of statements, as if to say, "you know?" Even the goddess, Arlene, does it now. ("Valley Girl" talk, I'm told it is called.) It is emitted by the same younger set that emits "ah" for "ee" and "eh" vowels, like their jaws were falling off from beriberi. I hate that phony crap. Or, 7), doctors' receptionists that rattle-off-what-they-are-calling-for-like-a-machine-gun-as-if-it-were-in-French-which-may-as-well-be-in-French-which-has-little-inflection. Did you know? Oh, and here is a habit that burns my kiester, which by the way, developed a hemorrhoid driving all the way back from Iowa last weekend and elicited and "Over the weekend!?" from my gastroenterologist, and answering 8) "That's correct" to questions! It can only be answered to statements; else there is nothing to be correct about. I heard Barrack Obama do it the other day. And how about: 9) "No problem" instead of, "you're welcome." Thank you very much." "No problem." Well, hell! I know there is no damned PROBLEM!

Ah, what the hell. Why get bogged down with what my brother-in-law would call all this prose crap. At this rate it could last longer than a PDQ Bach fugue. I hate:

1. The national embarrassment known as a congressional hearing.
2. Over-programmed kids.

3. The way we dress, me included.

4. Cuties in the public, now pubic eye, following the lead of the Doris Day types, being America's perfect little prick teasers too long. They have to pull sexy publicity stunts to show how real they are. Example: Jennifer Aniston's side boob shot on the magazine cover now that she isn't America's TV sweetheart anymore and going to be a REAL actress. So haul 'em out, Honey.

5. Women in the public eye whose validity is measured in cleavage inches and boob angles and dimensions.

6. The fact that I like seeing these things.

7. Women in the public eye that try so hard to have big ones when they don't.

8. The truly miniscule vocal talent most pop singers truly have, usually showing the same cleavage. Even if male: to wit…

9. Those disgusting former commercials of John Basedow: why doesn't he just invest in a good bra.

10. That the world actually prefers a mediocre or poor singing voice to a great one.

11. The hordes of people in the public eye that cannot pronounce "nuclear."

12. Calling people who execute Rap "artists."

13. Saying "anxious" when you mean "eager."

14. Cooking show hosts that have to refer to simmering food as "guys."

15. Cooking show hosts that have to refer to audience members as guys.

16. Waiters that call Arlene and me "guys."

17. "Ribbies" for RBIs by baseball announcers.

18. The culture that made the Super Bowl nipple possible, but the years of shock value that led up to the arena in which something like that was simply the next step.

19.Sports figures that cannot resist doing something to show the triumphan nature of what they just performed, even raising a finger in the air or clenching a fist. Where are the Joe DiMaggios and Stan Musials that humbly ran around the bases with their heads down, or that never even argued with the umpires?

20. Classical female concert pianists that can't come onstage fully dressed.

21. Emeril's use of the English language, embodying what every teacher since first grade tried to rid you—and him—of, the worst being, "What we're gonna do is we're gonna...." Jesus, man, just tell us what the frick it is. And don't call it "guys" when you do.

22. Emeril.

23. Some people's perfumes. Jesus, God! I would rather smell cow shit than some of them. How can they stand such odors?

24. Busboys that have to slam dishes into their tubs like human wrecking balls.

25. "Twenty-four-seven."

26. Redundancies: "Separate out, return back, distill down, add in."

27. Bicycle delivery boys going down the wrong direction of the street in New York City, especially silently and with no light at night, expecting you to see them.

28. Local news team banter.

29. The utter fools college basketball coaches make of themselves during games.

30. People who have to shout at each other in restaurants.

31. Our utter plasticity and materialism, leaving some prominent people, like Matt Drudge, stunned when a new "Holy Father" said it before one Christmas. What planet have these apes been on?

32. That a pope is any holier a father than anyone else.

33. That he is called any kind of father.

34. How fat we are.

35. Radio shows that fade in and out with "bumper" music that makes it harder to hear what is being said.
36. The absolutely disgusting way cook show hosts pronounce the names of the foreign dishes they make and wines that go with them. And this is expertise?
37. Academy Awards that do the same, not that I watch.
38. Sit-coms.
39. Everything else on TV except the History Channel.
40. February pronounced like FebUary, even in the dictionary.
41. People that show from their questions and actions toward me that they recognize me as old. Example: "Are you retired?" "Sir, do you need help?"
42. That waitress at Shoney's who gave me a senior discount without my asking.
43. Cashiers who ask if I need any help getting my groceries to/in the car.
44. Having to eat breakfast when I am not hungry just because Arlene hits the floor like a Tsunami at 6 a.m., ravenous by 8.
45. Having to press anything on a damned ATM machine in this country to speak English.
46. Interviewers and show hosts who can't let their guests talk without interruption.
47. Gyms.
48. People who don't listen to their messages and read their emails.
49. Overexposed public figures.
50. One more picture of Oprah.
51. Public figures getting up and telling their cutesy little drug addiction stories.
52. Any pop singer ever again that grabs his—or her—crotch.
53. The moan, grunt and whine style of pop singing that is in now, sounding like Snowhite getting it for the first time. I guess they learned it from pro tennis players.
54. Young couples standing around, like shopping at Sam's Club or the Metropolitan Museum, with their arms around each other and their hands down each other's pants.

55. The fact that I am too old to have anybody want me to do that anymore.
56. The fact that I am too old to want to do that anymore.
57. The fact that I am old enough to want to put the last two in print.
58. People (strangers) that use the "F" word loudly where other strangers, including women and children, hear it.
59. People, even in speeches, starting off in third person and ending in first person plural before the sentence is over: "The American people will always do what *we* have to do to succeed."
60. "Cut" a check instead of write one.
61. The air that is in a toothpaste tube.
62. Clerks that involve me in their daily troubles and other conversations with each other.
63. Clerks who are good at one main thing: being implacably unhurryable.
64. People in restaurants that hover over me waiting for a nearby table or leaving, with the cracks of their asses inches from my food.
65. Recorded messages telling me the number I called is busy when I can hear the busy signal just fine. Duh.
66. Duh.
67. ANY music playing in my ear when I am on hold.
68. Recorded messages on my cell phone service telling me TWICE that the message waiting for me has not been heard. Jesus, God. Just play it.
69. People who don't curb their dogs in NYC.
70. People that don't clean up after their curbed or uncurbed dogs.
71. The Rolling Gall Stones.
72. Baseball players who run slower toward first base than any other.
73. Baseball managers and front office personnel who won't enforce a correction of the problem.
74. That we have to go around EVERYWHERE with something stuck in our ears, programmed, stimulated and zoned out.

75. Why pop singers have to look so pained when they sing. It is for me to look pained. Combined that look with a jaw jutting out and you know you are in for some painful noise.

76. That they all use the exact same stupid-assed, little vocal and musical scoops and ornaments. It's so boring.

77. The fact that everyone can't have the same great taste that I have.

78. Celebrities (I suppose) who pronounce their own names in a correct way linguistically, yet butcher all other words in that same language: ex., "Fieri."

79. Celebrities (pre-supposed) and native speakers of languages that overdue certain of their favorite words: "Pancitta," instead of "pancetta."

80. "Spot on."

81. Anything like the Rolling Gall Stones.

82. "At the end of the day."

83. "Moving forward."

84. That these things catch on so easily.

85. "Sign *off*" on something instead of "sign."

86. Waiters that have to announce their names to me before serving me.

87. Food professionals who cannot say the correct names of what they are cooking.

88. *Sommeliers* who cannot say the correct names of the wines they are recommending.

89. Food industry professionals who can't say either one correctly.

90. Our complexes that dictate not wanting them said correctly.

91. The level to which the Food and Cooking networks have sunk.

92. ForMIDable and appLICable.

93. Hearing three classical concert pianists billed as the three "hottest" pianists.

94. Seeing the same pianists—and others—come onstage dressed like whores.

95. Greensboro drivers who drive like their car bumpers are having sex with mine.

96. People who complain all the time.

Good morning, good afternoon and good night. Have a nice day without no problem.

OLD POPES NEVER DIE, JUST FADE FROM PEW

OR

THE INSTANT-BULL, CONSTANTIN-POPAL CONFLAP

Ecles./File MCLVXIII-XLVXXLM:XLT-LARIAT/4X4
sub/froth:vati-rndup:vulcan//bs.popeshtsfactusgod-e:yegads

The curtain rises on God, seated at the right hand of Himself, but left of the upstage center double doors. He is wearing a baseball cap, Keds tennis shoes, cutoffs and a T-shirt reading: "I'm a Magician, not a Beautician" *across the front. He seems slightly annoyed, looking at his watch, patting his right Ked.*

A few supers stand at the exits and at times meander around. One smallish elderly lady works at an easel, doing a charcoal of a small reddish bird. She stands when Pete enters.

Pete, entering from stage right, crosses left, addresses God directly, looking slightly red in the face.

Pete. This next one's tricky.

God. Who is it?

Pete. That guy. You know. That *guy*.

G. Oh. I've been dreading it. Okay, show him in.

Popal. (*Enters, crossing to center; addresses God directly with a wavering gesture*): "Gran Dio."

G. Keep your hand down and stop stirring up the air. I designated that sign for the Native American long before you were born.

P. I see. Well...I am most happy to finally mee....

G. Yes, yes, I know......I know. (*Waits, then continues*). You puzzle me, you know that? You really do.

P. Sire?

G. Do you realize you impersonate me; do you? (*Pauses*). I always liked you and I don't doubt you did some good but...you do.

P. Seigneur?

G. Don't call me that. I am God. You of all people ought to know that if I have gender I can't be God. At least have the good sense to call me "Father-Mother." Didn't you read the *Da Vinci Code?* You guys set civilization back hundreds of years with all that "Father In Heaven" stuff.

P. I see. Well, that's different from.....

G. And where did you get off blessing and forgiving people? Only I do that, get it? Granted, it's almost automatic, but there are some things I like to do for myself. Capisc?

P. I thought.... I mean, I knew that You, well...

G. I know what you thought! Did you ever once wonder at my wanting my people bothered, going around thinking and talking, let alone obsessing, on me all the time? **ALL** the time? I never asked for that, never designated a professional "God" person, a "God major." (*Chuckles*).

(Continuing). I mean, I gave you life, right? What was there to enjoy in what you did? All that time on your knees, trying to reach me. I never asked that of you. Those infernal weekly get-together things with all that…that…stuff. Think of all the hip replacements. Have you seen the medical device stock lately? One day it's bear, then instant bull. I hate that term, "bear" market anyway. It causes people out in Jersey to start shooting the poor things. Wouldn't be a problem if the Orthodox guys up in the Catskills'd stop feeding them.

//

(Rises, and takes few steps, paces a little, turns back to P).

(Resumes). You know what my design was? I wanted to know if someone simply *believed* in me, then go out, for Christ's sake, and have a good time. And who was your tailor? What's that smoking thing you walk in circles with, boinking those poor sons-o-bitches in the balls with, all the good folk sitting out there shivering! For years, yet, in the days when there was no heat, let alone antibiotics. Who would do something like that? You really think I care anything about all that nonsense?

//

(Continuing). I mean, for once really think about it! You say things by rote that people have been repeating for a thousand years. How can that have meaning? Besides, don't you know second hand smoke is bad for you? And them? What were you thinking? What's the purpose of that thing, anyway? You guys can't even make up your mind what language to navigate in.

P. But in all due respect, I know those people wanted to sit there, feeling their connection with You. They came away better for it. Think of all the sightings of the Virgin Mary around Cincinnati and Northern Kentucky alone that the people rush out to see like a bunch of banshees, using all their gas? Don't you call that believing, especially at these pump prices?

G. Mary who? What virgin? And whose bright idea was it you should live alone with a bunch of guys, wearing all those flowing things? …. // Let me put it this way: After I made Adam, what did I do?

P. Rested? On the seventh day?

G. No! Eve! I made Eve. Whose idea was it that you couldn't indulge in some fleshy pleasures once in a while? Look at all the problems it's been causing! It's degenerate. It's your rules, not mine; I never asked you to do that. Besides, you took vows of, what's that word: "celibacy," not chastity. Chastity's for nuns.

P. Well. Uh… There's something you ought to….er, I should adm….

G. And look at all the prostate problems! That organ is one of my minor flaws anyway. You whackos didn't help any.

P. It's sort of like this….uh..

G. Wait your turn, holy man. I take a nap one afternoon and wake up to find you guys slaughtering each other for three centuries, over that, that… what is it? That "three" thing. That triad idea….

P. The Trinity?

G. I guess so.

P. But Your Holiness…

G. Stop that I tell you! That's your invention. //

(*Continuing*). Boy, that three thing. Which one of you clowns came up with that? You do know how to carry on. Drive it right into the ground. I'd rather you had a date at a Sonic Drive-In once in a while. It's not natural your way. And that guy they put in after you. What's that stupid name they gave him? Dominic Polaris, Benedictine Brandy or something. He's always kneeling down there where he thinks you are! In the front of that big building; the one with all the people waiting for cannoli outside. Hell, the way you guys go on, he'll be up here before they figure out if he was even a NAZI or not. I had to laugh, though, when he said all those other religions were "insufficient."

(*Pauses*). Sometimes it doesn't even pay to get up of a century.

P. You mean the cathedral nave?

G. Whatever. Cryptic place, that. And you aren't even there! // Well, are you? What's he doing *there*? Honestly, they—or you, I guess. I don't really get how these things work—but they could have gone for a little younger guy, don't you think?
(*Continuing*). I mean, with all they give you credit for, do you know what the biggest change in the church was during your lifetime? Electricity!

P. I am beginning to think....

G. All right, all right. I said I liked you; you just, I don't know, got kind of goofy on me. Think what you could have done and with all that money! I liked you best when you walked around the woods in your khakis and white shirt. That's where I was; you found me there. Nature, you know? It's your True Nature. Everyone's really.

But right now I want you to take some time, get to know the other half; get your head together. I think I'm going to cast you...

P. In your own image, Sire?

G. There you go again. No, cast you together with ...

P. Into **HELL**!? Please! I always tried...

G. No, not that!! You know what this "hell" thing was that you guys made so much of? It was a garbage pit!! A stinking hole outside the gates of Jerusalem. That's what they called them, "Hell!" They had to do something with all the stuff, right? I think Amadeus called it "Hoelle Rache"* or some such May have been the Mason thing. But that was the name of it and you bozos, I don't know, made up this metaphor, this big deal of it like there were people in it or *something*; burning people with the garbage I guess.

      (Continuing). What an asinine notion. What kind of monster do you think I am? I'd have to be a terrorist to do something like *that*, course you didn't really go so far as to say I would cut their throats. Besides, what is there to burn if it's only a soul?

//

      (Continuing). Don't you get it? I love everyone the same. Besides, if I made them, how could they be bad? It's the mind of man that gets the whole thing screwed up. It's all an illusion anyway. Hell, I even loved Schickelgruber.

P. Who? //////…///// Oh. No! Not him?!

G. Yeah, him. He's around here somewhere. Pete, where's Adolf? Someone wants to meet him. *(Back to the Popal)*. He was one of your predecessors, you know. The short time one; didn't have to do it long. You know the one…

P. HUH? Pope Pau….was .. Hitl …. How could he ha….b. He was too young!
Do You have any water? Unblessed is fine, well obviously, I guess... Oh, my. May I sit?

G. Big whoopee! That's not the way it works. Like veterinarians say, you're thinking in human terms. There's no such thing as chronology in heaven. What have you been studying all this time. Pete, get him some

---

*Title of Mozart's "Queen of the Night" aria in his opera The Magic Flute

milk. Whole milk is fine; there's nothing wrong with it. He needs fat along with protein. That's what I made Lipitor and Lactaid for. (*Waits*).

(*Continues*). Now look, pull yourself together and go down to the end of the hall on the left. The room on the right is for Bill and Monica. They'll be in the Ecstasy Room. Don't pay any attention when they get here and don't bother them. The things they have to work out are different from yours. They're worse, just not garbled like you, know-what-they-want kind of thing, you know. They'll get it: hand rolled Churchill, maduro Cuban seed with Connecticut wrapper. Castro likes 'em. He'll be up here soon, so I laid in a supply. Be hell straightening that place out after him. And him himself! Course, it's better than a bunch of rag hea.....never mind.

(*Continues*). Anyway, I got some babes waiting for you. But the left side, you hear? And you see that little lady over there by the door? She is your guide. Her name is Wilma Lynch. It rhymes with "finch," that's how you can remember it. Ask her about anything, but I'd stay away from baptism.

P. You don't mean you have some of those, well, vestal virgi..?

G.   NOW LISTEN: THERE'LL BE NONE OF THAT CRAP! THERE IS NOTHING LIKE THAT AROUND HERE! OR ANYWHERE ELSE, YOU HEAR? THAT'S THAT OTHER BOLOGNA. I'VE GOT MY HANDS FULL WITH THOSE LUNATICS. VESTAL VIRGINS!! AT LEAST YOU GUYS....well..

P.   Abstained? We did better, didn't we?

G. If I have to say. But I told you I didn't have any use for that either. Sometimes I look down there and think, "What the frick are these morons thinking?" Anyway, I want you to take some time before you go back. You could get it right in one more try if you just...

P. Go back? Go back!? You mean ... ...(he swallows). Uh, Mmm... Down..... *there?*

G. Of course. See how judgmental you are? Haven't you learned *any*thing?

P. But I always thought….. I devoted my whole life to….

G. I know. *(Sighs)*. You got that wrong too. Oh, and listen. If you ever do one of those stadium things again…

P. Mass, of course *(Coughs)*.

G. Whatever. Use the other one next time.

P. Signo… I mean I beg your pardon?

G. The *visitor's* dugout, lummox. Serves you right with all the trouble you guys got into up in Boston.

P. You don't mean to tell me….

G. It figures. Just figures. Right in the middle of it and you don't get it. The whole world knows God's a Yankee fan but you. It's the winningest franchise in history. You think I'd throw my support to an inferior organization? Pitching sucks right now, but… And the Boss better go easy with the firings before next season. Mel's already had it. And I'm worried about center field.

P. You? Calling someone else "the Bo…"

G. The other Boss, then, holy man… See what I mean? No imagination.
Now get outta here. It's the third inning already. Oh, and the library's up there too. Look under Dan Brown. It'll get the ball rolling for you.

Blackout as Popal reaches for support. God heads for the exit. CURTAIN!

Artist's Digest And The Classical American Popsicle

Turn past the prayer response and let the sermon begin; you'll disagree anyway. Maybe you have all along. Consider, at least, a vote for some knee-slapping entertainment.

And give me this: we've all wondered what our world would be like without the assassination of John F. Kennedy, or certain social movements and global confrontations. When it comes to music, though, I venture to say that few have given such thought *much* thought; for example, Elvis' or the Beatles' having never appeared on the scene to send along the various levels of turning on, tuning out, and for my take on it, tanking completely.

Granted, I'm at an age where everything looks worse than that which came before, especially values, much like that song from the era in which decent Music Theater inhabited the halls, "Kids! I don't Know What's Wrong With These Kids Today!"

Of course, if I were king, I would abolish anything not an asset to society, period, according to the doctrine of me and my crown. Among the rejects would be rock and rap "music," screen violence polluting the atmosphere, and ninety-eight percent of television. Does that mean the only governmental hope is a benign dictatorship? But of course, that's a contradiction in terms.

Most people over forty are today perennial anachronisms, feeling their way through a sea of confound-ment: full-flowered people in a fully flowering age of irresponsible "truthlessness," characterized by indolent oafs zoning out in front of some type of monitor or other, serving notice of breakups by means of text messages.

The first time I noticed a discrepancy for the specific twine I intend to here unravel, was in the artist studio of someone I dated briefly in the mid-1970s. The walls of our current abode are to this day peppered with her artworks, well, in between those now of my own. She did oils, charcoals, watercolors, cutting and pasting, and who knows what else with techniques acquired mostly since that time.

And so it was, interesting that is, watching the classy creativity taking place in her studio, well, except for the rock music accompanying the cultural emerging forms. When I pointed out the discrepancy between the two realms, I think she was a little stunned. But I had a point.

Early in my artistic life, I had learned a lesson. I was part of an organization named Affiliate Artist, Inc., born outside the City, but which sprang to maturity inside, where so many endeavors advance to adulthood. I have considered what the organization accomplished in the thirty or so years since I participated, and concluded that it was good.

Yet, I can't help but wonder where it is that it shows. Especially given our latter day definition of music, where are the hundreds of children alone with whom I shared my vocal art? Have their lives been affected by what I gave them, even once I explained certain things to them?

"A singer is a later maturing athlete," I told them, warming up my voice while they entered the room, squealing at the sounds I was making. "Them" was every single fourth, fifth and sixth grader in the town of Jackson, Tennessee, school year 1975-76, once the local powers saw that I could handle large groups. Where are those kids now, and do they even remember?

And I spread my oral wings before larger, if not more sophisticated, assemblages: churches, concert halls, shopping malls, and arts festivals, where blended all kinds of elevated examples. At one of them, my coordinator asked me within earshot of a handful of enthusiasts, what I would like to do, since my program was over: go home or to the ballet performance. Turning up my nose at the idea of watching dance, I showed the mother of the day's prima ballerina how broad-based I wasn't, while she showed me her manners by not dishing what I deserved.

During the following summer, that of 1976, I sublet a friend's apartment on Manhattan's Upper West Side. As penance for my *faux pas* in Tennessee, I scoured the terpsichorean presentations of New York. In every type of location I could find, from fourth floor attics, to the Metropolitan Opera, I attended examples of dance, until personally enchanted by the art form. If my resume said I was an artist or other esthete, then I needed to be so across the board.

*

In what should be a similar realm, with the exception of the fine taste of one John Batchelor, radio talk show hosts forever blast rock music, or that synthetic "chopstick" stuff, as their "bumper" music returning after a commercial. Surely, head-on collisions of the two-party system notwithstanding, there is little disagreement in that what these celebrities do with their lives is more akin to "classical" than "colloquial," of erudition rather than mere physical stimulation, and requiring ongoing formal learning. Yet, their taste in music is the lowest of all two-legged upright species.

Raise your hands. Anyone see a discrepancy there? No? I am failing you.

Did you know that at one time the only extant music in the western world—at least except for certain forms of religious and folk music—was what would now be termed "classical," or "serious?" It is the same genre that school youths congregating on the platforms of New York subways, and not long ago driven out by during a social experiment, call "old people's music."

To be sure, serious music varied greatly from century to century, also from vocal to instrumental, and sacred to secular. With each new epoch, composers- seeking to expand on what had come before- were regularly condemned by the guardians of the old school. So too were the trends in visual arts, such as that hideously vulgar approach to dabbing paint specks upon a canvas known as *Impressionism*. Its equal in music, they didn't like Debussy's assays either. Imagine a music world without his, *or* Ravel's contributions!

But that basic *level* of music was pretty much what there was, and has, moreover, survived to this day, proving from the test of time alone, its worth. Do forgive me; the "Golden Oldies" of pop do appear on regular airwave blasts devoted to them and, speaking of old peoples' taste, are to be lauded, compared to what they led to.

Classic and/or serious works, though, are loved by people of all ages who have the sensibilities to appreciate them no matter how many times they experience them, whether as fare for orchestra, opera, architecture, or the dignified wall cover of multi-million dollar edifices known as museums.

Unfortunately, those people are not what today constitutes anything approaching a majority. My favorite professor said it was because classical music wasn't meant for the masses. But I wonder:

would it have been the same had not the other types of organized sounds reared their mostly ugly heads?

Nor was there an absence of rowdy-friend entertainment connected with the (serious) music of other centuries. Overtures to operas, in fact, were mainly written to quiet the gaming noises emanating from tables set up about the halls. Today we take alternate routes. With the popular, more noisy and vulgar forms of the "art," or so it would seem, go their own distinct strata of human walks of life.

Would, at the memorial service of Tim Russert—a public figure I admired—that such taste (mine) had been in place for the strains that reached the neo-Gothic crevices of the Washington Cathedral, known to me as the venue where I performed such masterworks as the Verdi *Requiem*, and Beethoven's *Missa Solemnis*. So Tim and Bruce Springsteen had become friends. Did that make Bruce's "song" appropriate in such a setting? Of course, you say, why not? But then I am ruined, schooled to look down on, practicing my art in dozens of inspiring physical venues as well, and thereby repeatedly catapulted to much greater heights, both literal and figurative. To me it was a sacrilege.

Indeed it never ceases to amaze me how people will gather around any scraggly-looking semi-upright *Homo sapiens* clutching a guitar, striking, and little more than crowing like a sexually deprived rooster along with it. Yet, the most personally scurrilous thing relative to "music" of this nature is that in doing so anyone should ever automatically assume it is my taste; that walking into a drug store, I would be one of the targets, someone placated, let along titillated, by that kind of sound enough to purchase more product; or, waiting on the telephone to my doctor's office, that the not-so-brief interlude is more tolerable with such effrontery.

Indeed there is too much going on with us anyway and the best thing that could possibly happen is more often total quiet, and that if music were performed, it should be worthy of being listened to, concentrated upon alone. Quality music, like its equal in culinary arts, should be taken in thinking on little else. But again, I am therein ruined. I am an artistic *foodie*.

We recently had a president who professed preference for a certain rock screamer. Let me see, was it the Grateful Deadheads or, that—what was his name—Ozzie something-or-other, one of the recently dried-out (again) goons from a topnotch rehab program which he had no trouble affording. As much as President Bush is disliked, shouldn't his association with such a "thing" along be enough to blast it to the outer reaches of what could finally be called civilization? Oh well, I have even heard that we now have a congressional rock band to go along with the president's. No veto power will for once be necessary therein, since the two sides might actually agree.

When it comes to the names of these creeps (rockers), I smugly don't do well. Psychologists call it repression. I recently saw a blurb in the NY Post, complete with picture of "singer" Amy Weinstock or Winehead or Winebreath or Brainsoak, in London, torching a preternaturally long cancer stick upon the steps of the very hospital from which she had just alighted, accompanied by the oh! so stern warning that further damage done her by the likes of ANY foreign substance, including tobacco, would not only ruin her so-called voice, but the rest of her emaciated body. She didn't; and it did. Maybe it is as they say of geldings just *after* the knife: their last wing-ding is not only their last, but their best.

Sports figures, on occasion, are allowed to select favorite music to be played for the assembled folding-chair masses, as the players themselves come to bat, or are honored, etc. Nor am I ever surprised by the sounds I hear, just before turning the sound down on the TV. I am likely to tolerate a "Soul" version of some exotic tune, distance myself relocating to the kitchen when I hear the same lowlife pop I battle at the grocer's, hit the mute button for "acid rock," but throw a ball-peen hammer through my newly- purchased HD wide screen for "rap."

But as much as I love sports and wish I could have been good enough to be professional, I don't really expect anything musically aristocratic from these highly gifted, disciplined beings. After all, we were lucky enough to have had Robert Merrill sing the nation anthem from time to time at Yankee Stadium, and later his recording of same after he was past his prime, or engaged elsewhere.

I am more dismayed at the professionals who *announce* these same activities. Fairly early on, I learned that what even broadcasters call music can only mean a certain level that I scant allude to by that title. Mostly, I force myself to say "it's okay;" after all they're not broadcasting from the sound booth of the Sidney Opera House. At this increasing level of ubiquity, though, I marvel at where symphony and opera audiences come from, even in their moribund state, and am never in the least surprised to hear when one such organization bites the dust. *C'est la vie, e c'est* the age we live in.

I am likewise sure to have made known my belief that the single greatest enemy we political animals have is the two-party system itself. There are topics that I am conservative about, liberal for others, although I curiously notice that being a person of formal education, I am assumed to be *leftist* on all degrees of the sundial. My blood is red, but a prude I *ain't*. I have had my dalliances, though by today's standards, negligible. Most of all, I resent having it thought that I either have, or need to have, my opinions formed by a so-called party, or its "platform." As I surely have said previously, to me the two-party system is the real problem anyway.

From the same enlightened sources that inform my differing impulses from the primitive, the mental, the emotional, the high-level artistic, all the way to the base, I know there exists as strong a difference between doing something privately, even habitually, and the wholesale manufacture and marketing of it, such as sex. As one of my teachers said to a rather, shall we say, "loose" student of hers who challenged her status as a sexual being, "Oh I like sex too; but I'm a connoisseur."

Ergo, as sure as I breathe, I know that there is no, *nada, niente, ingen,* and *nichts* good to come of the over-stimulated practices of our current western civilization, growing hourly, and that pop, hard rock and so-called "hip-hop" head the list of what should be Johnny-Come-Nevers.

*

Taking it all to a head, I once read an article the New York Sun on the subject of a recently-retiring super curator of the Museum Of Modern Art. John had had a distinguished career and done great things for MOMA. After a considerable rough beginning as my next-door neighbor, being on friendly terms with him was special. True, I could occasionally detect a sort of snobbish truncation of passing conversations about art, such as when I would refer to such-and-such Museum as being in the wrong city. Be that as it may, I am passionate about visual art and seldom pass on an opportunity to pick the brains of an expert.

The patching of the wall linking our two apartments had been constructed poorly, and the occasion of John's well nigh melting down our doorbell and shouting obscenities about how the "noise" from our singers would ruin their dinner parties, no doubt caught him at a bad time. After all, one can only take so much culture before needing to blow out the cobs. I do understand that. The same goes for the worn-out Patsy Cline albums that accompanied the referred-to parties. He was most generous getting us tickets to the wonderful Matisse/Picasso exhibit in Queens that he himself had hung, and he and his significant other donated several nice items to us when they moved out. We really, truly, miss them.

I was nevertheless not in the least surprised at the apparent lavishness of the banquet held in the man's honor as he stepped down from his prestigious position with MOMA, or the tone of the festivities. Surely it was a black tie affair, replete with esthetes and other experts, eloquent speeches and the like, all fitting for, and leading up to, the Jasper Johns miniature, presented to John in recognition of his manifold contributions, to say nothing of his hard-fought knowledge in the field of classic modern art.

Would that I could have been a fly on the wall, surely reminding me in art world terms of what John F. Kennedy said on the subject of human gray matter to an American Phi Beta Kappa conference at the White House. Quipped the president, "There hasn't been so much intelligence assembled under this roof since Thomas Jefferson dined here alone." Ditto an amount in culture, taste, erudition, and artistic savvy as on the MOMA occasion, including as well the evening's musical accompaniment, chosen by the man of the hour himself.

What, then, *was* the laudatory, auditory theme for such an august affair?

No, not the piano sonatas of Mozart, nor an evening-long group of *Ländler* from the great German Romanticists; not the string quartets of Beethoven or the *Nocturnes* of Chopin. Absent too were such choices as the serenades of Brahms and Dvorak. This was, after all, *MOMA*, and presumably only twentieth (or later) century strains would be appropriate. Barber's famous adagio then? Close, but no cigar. The Grand Canyon Suite of Grofé, the early works of Berg and Schoenberg, or, being an easy-listening, feasting affair, perhaps the manifold melodies of one Sergei Rachmaninoff? Even the late French *Impressionists* would qualify. No?

If not these, then, only the works of a great champion of honesty in life and art himself would do, he not long issued from the, oh! so inspiring audience with Pope John Paul II, right after a hearty bout of Pontiff-admissions, including the subject's famous life-long attraction to self-destruction, standing, as it were, his own test of time, so that life-altering was His Holiness's cogent counsel: "Don't!"

So back to music, then who, was this figure, you say?

Why, you tiger, you! You guessed it! Who else? ….. Who but our very own native son …. … none other than …please join me in a round of applause for…. will the real twentieth century musical esthete please rise? My friends, welcome ……the one, the only………..Bob

Dyla

Wrens on my Yard Art

"Sculpture? What sculpture?"

You mean that thing in that yard? I thought it was a refuse pile. You been raking limbs getting ready for summer?

So let me get this straight: You're saying all you have to do is call something art, and it is? It doesn't have to be purchased, or at least have a price put on it? Hmm. Oh, like those orange flags stuck in the ground all over central park a few years ago? Hmmm, maybe I *am* an artist. You know that old quip, Gee, six munce uhgo I kuhdn't even spell technichian; now I are one!"

The chicken, the egg, the juice, the lemon, then the zest. But according to whom for what is the best? Is it, like Scotch and raw oysters, an acquired taste, or were we always meant to eat in some acquired order of another person's preference? Is it not how certain nationalities of foods derive? But why, because you like one set of tastes, do you find it as a basis for the loathing of another? Have you ever known one of those people who eat one thing at a time before going on? Disgusting!

Then too what part is actual art? As much as I love architecture, there is nothing to me like a living form to replicate. Look at all the painters though the ages that fixated on forms of the human body, especially female, that we wouldn't even consider beautiful today. Relative to my yard sculpture, I love the living; the feathered friends, more than the hard assemblages. The Carolina Wren was already a favorite of mine, not just since the earlier chapter, "A Finch in Time…," but from the ones that made it all the way to Ithaca, NY, and two years in a row built a nest in my leather nail pouch hanging in the barn. Sneaking into my garage and even kitchen now—here in their native home state—I have them (the wrens) to thank for not leaving my leftover popcorn to pepper the patio. Methinks some of this might just add up to the makings of art……

My business partner, Teddy, the one who screwed me to the point I will never completely recover financially, no matter how long I live, once turned down a family for renting the other side of his duplex in Astoria, NY, because he didn't want to smell curries cooking next door. He called them "Taliban," by the way. He also once suggested arson as a means of remedying our diner financial problems, referring to it as "Jewish Lightning." A self-styled food professional, he only knew some diner and some Greek dishes, usually by names he mispronounced. You get the idea of who was at fault in this little non-business, non-arrangement: me!

But now, just who really does constitute the, shall we say, "Quality Police," the ones who determine what such a thing even is, and why? One of my favorite answers regarding taste, culture, etc. is, "If you have to ask, telling you won't do any good." You either have it, or you don't.

How, then, do we substantiate these things? I am told that my stuff (you know, paintings, drawings, food dishes, singing, and my writing—ye gads!) are meant for a different market; one not local, not small town, not put before the public by some renegade band. In other words, it is higher of class. It sounds awfully arrogant, I know.

I suppose it is just another way of saying I am the black sheep of my family, having come from a such a location—herein previously described—and from which I obviously not only draw artistic material through the whole book to either prove or deny the main premise that I am a straining absentee gardener!

I once read a piece of mine aloud to all of my remaining and extended family members, only to notice THEY didn't notice. I kind of trailed off reading, not that it changed anything either way. Another instance saw my recitation to Arlene's side of the family get a head start on a good night's sleep.

On another occasion, though, my missive hit a better mark. I wrote to my (small town/county) high school superintendent, long after he had retired, telling him that when I came home for a visit and saw him, I was aware of being in the presence of greatness, and that, By God, I was glad to be a country boy! His son was Secretary of Education for the State of Missouri and personally wrote me to say what I great thing I had done for his father. I remember *his* father for, among many other things, having convened school assemblies to talk about such issues as teenage pregnancies, of which there was a rash there in the late 1950s. Now it seems as if we hardly notice those things.

Coming full circle, I'm not sure if there is any marketable art in all of this, so why did I even talk about it, or write my superintendent to start with, especially since my artistic creations are supposed to be a notch above? Would he understand? Would my parents have? Does it matter, or even help refine the definition of said art? Faulkner must have dealt with similar mental discussions.

Of course, the way I have been shooting off my mouth this whole book, why would I suddenly balk at looking arrogant? Perhaps, being an artist of yet another recent sort (painting), it's on my brain. I haven't quite as yet even published (this) my magnum opus, or sold paintings the way I thought I would. People rave about the works I post here and there, but none so far have backed up the compliment, or legitimized the personal but otherwise empty rave review. But I do seem to see a lot around me that begs the question of what art is; few that answer it. After all, we call almost anything "beautiful" or "great," yet by the name of "professional" only when it has entered into an exchange of currency, no matter how bad it is. I think we may just be getting to the bottom of this little vignette's topic......

Pulling up to the gate, the question still remains: what does all of the above mean art really is, and what should I do? Call this chapter "Wrens On My Junk Pile" or "The Birds Newest Roost," even "Can't you copulating idiots put your money where your mouth is?" Maybe I should just consider that my junk will eventually go the same route of appraisal as other works I see scattered about? Then again, why not forget all about it and move somewhere like South America where I might be able to live on my Social Security, paint and write for the sheer love of it, uncontaminated by mixing business and pigments?

To tell the truth, I really have looked into teaching a little jungle English as a second language as well, while there, to help subsidize the aforementioned expensive—in that case—hobby. After all, I have periodically dealt with people who thought singing too was just exercising one's God-given talent; that I should go out and get a real job. Well, I sang a few times for free, but don't think I tried any less hard to do it well. I wonder: does that make me more—or less— professional?

So on and on, as my paintings hang here on the walls, probably in the balance too, even within ear—or ether—shot of a plethora of generously-complimenting people I know that have those greenbacks ready to roll out of any bodily pouch without noticing. My yard sculpture, you see, has a slight green tint to it from the pressure treatment meant to preserve it. Still, I am not sure I have painted with that general color (green) very often: maybe do it as a hint? Am I coming around and *veritas* psychobabbling the way I did in the hospital after surgery?

I just love **writing myself into** some posture. Plus, Arlene would be proud of me since the corner I have written myself into has been her idea all along. It's great to be appreciated by a long-time companion. If only she would come to South America with me! Of course, if I were the ongoing musical and didactic artist she is, I wouldn't either. And here is the real ass-burner: she earns a living at it. Oh no! I just blew my whole theory. Well, not really, considering the times I have seen her passed over in favor of lesser talents and human specimens.

For what it is worth, I always wanted to ask my ex-father-in-law if, after his many years as a prominent psychologist, he thought intelligence could really be measured. Now it seems to be moving like the movie, "The Blob" to include talent. Likewise, it would be oh so interesting to enter into a discussion with *his* father, long time Dean of Education at University of Missouri, about the vagaries of classroom learning. He was the first I knew to say, "Here is your degree; now go out and get your education." Together the two of them alone read enough books to not only redefine intelligence and education, but also form a yard sculpture the size of an average American county.

As I've held forth before and should now wind down with, my main high school English teacher, the ever strict and straight-laced Miss Booth, wanted me to major in that very subject. I could tell, even though I made poor grades in her classes; she knew I had the goods. I think I should have. One doesn't get (or expect) money for English lesson plans, on which to place categorical stamps of approval. Ergo, do stay tuned for my last and most important flash-frozen views on edification, life's choices, and of, not "Zen and the Art of Archery," but "Truth in Yard Art." There may yet be some sooth in this sayer's final observations.

Mastering "Lie", "Lay," and "Lain"

The picture is, by now, clear. Though never having so much as smoked a single joint, I'm a wild thing, many of them, in fact, hand-rolled into one. If reduced to a stream of consciousness blur, which happens, my thoughts would conform to the Finger Lakes, or the Stockholm Archipelago I once sailed in, even walked on in winter.

I cannot guess if my reader knew much about classical singers before this book, or if such will be the case afterward: a self-absorbed, high-maintenance lot are we, as susceptible to unfiltered flattery as any sub-species ever to stand upright. Most would kill for voices that are both large and beautiful. One or the other is easy to achieve; both is difficult.

There is an in-house joke people say to singers they had best know well: "Your voice is small but ugly." In the same vein, I will iterate a final time that, though a bad husband and father, I was at least an equally bad high school student.

Still other lunacy lurks. I was never blocked from subsequently appreciating something—or someone—that I didn't take good advantage of earlier, finding use for figures of the past when others stuck to their guns as long as spite was "musterable." My opinions, as I got older, changed: the strictest professors became the good ones; but then, I am "old school," even the previously noted "old fuck." Just ask anyone, then thank her for the compliment.

When Miss Booth growled at me as I whizzed through that pronoun quiz, I knew we liked each other. She must have known me better than I did. Running into her on my hometown square days before I began college, she read like Silas Marner when I let slip what my major was to be. Of course, she was probably tone deaf.

I have had the previously cited habit of dashing letters off to people that, in retrospect, had become mentors. Miss Booth was one. Inconsistent with my lifelong attitude toward tardiness, I pointed out to her that finally mastering "lie," "lay," and "lain" was better than never. As she would know, most don't: "lay" is surely the most misused word in the English language, lying simply people's most salient trait, at least contemporaneously. Normally I try not to do either: misuse "lay," or lie.

In this—what came to be—the *book's* witching hour, possibly also that of my writing career, I must forthwith admit to a mastery of "lie" on another level: the sense in which what is a partial truth, that which you perfunctorily assume to be so, or that which merely seems a harmless untruth, is just another lie. Because you utter something innocently doesn't mean it isn't a falsehood, just as, by the way, because you think you have good reason for doing it.

Likewise, anytime you have been too lazy to research something enough to state it truthfully in writing...

Tibor, my best professor—the one they hate to this day—said something to me in passing: if you want to become expert in a subject you know nothing about, *write a book on it.* It sounds stupid and quite un-bookworthy, but, in fact, is true. Combine that with my long time hang-up about truthfulness and you have my one and only book, yea at this very point in time. I simply didn't have the gumption to start over.

Like grammar, birds and baptism, the quality of truth was another of my mother's legacies, whether I always lived up to it or not. Only, the kind of lie I am thinking of now lies in another realm from what she would have understood. I think Miss Booth did:

Not knowing yourself is just another form of lying. Not sufficiently pushing through to your true self a bigger one, never finding it the biggest lie of all.

To my delayed and dubious credit, I no longer fool around the way I did back in the Geneva/Vienna days. Rather, I've been fooling myself, if messing with your mind instead. Perhaps it was because the topic for the book seemed catchy, or marketable. I don't "lay" to you, but no longer "lie down on the job" not telling you. Neither am I fibbing, crossing my fingers or "storying." I have been lying, flat lying to you, though it took the whole book to come to it, itself just another measly untruth. If you feel cheated, write to me at garykendall575@gmail.com for a refund, but first lend your ear for a final cut.

Friends, Romans and kids: when you don't apply yourself to an early and fundamental course of study, other people realize things you don't. You rationalize. You yourself may not know, or care, if you have aptitude; to you you're just dumb or think you have a calling elsewhere. After a while, you're in such a rut you're not even sure if you're making an effort.

Being a seasoned world traveler is only one form of education for which you may play catch up. If you don't exercise your young brain, you never stop "busting" your chops; you've dulled your future senses. Your self-assessments, that which you have concluded to be the real you, are based on false data.

Yea, though, I tread on sandy terrain.

Public school learning could be compared to what they say about youth in general: wasted on the you-know-what. You are a youthful hack; not savoring, not imbued with the same "charge" from something new the way you will later when those things—indeed most things—mean more. You need a lesson from KoKo: as if conscious of her scant nine years, exulted at each tiny piece of foliage along the way from the truck seat.

Here I am, jack of too many trades, clueless what to do when, no, *if,* I grow up. Despite the pressure to the contrary, college students who take several semesters to determine a major are right so to do; they should make a process of it, taking, like "Sky King," a whole lot more, in this case, time.

Which is better, early or late blooming?

Only you can answer, and according to your accrued beliefs: what you do and don't do, have done and have not done, what you will thirst for, based on a lifelong satiety or dearth. But I would hazard that something about grass will continue to be of a different hue over yonder, though you just merged from that particular Laughing Place.

Life happens while you are making plans.

From where I strap myself to an upright position, one of the great shames is taking a whole existence to know who you are, though one could actually do worse. Not *ever* finding the phantom you would be the greater tragedy. Ah, but growing nearer the end, you don't have so much time—time *or* energy—to make something of the precious dawn to which you have awakened. How often people yearn for youth, knowing what they "now" know. It ain't gonna happen, though some "present" with the smarts in the early rounds. It is a fraternity for which I was never rushed.

Write a book and you will learn.....perhaps to thine own self to be true.

You, reader, have helped me divine that I should *never* have been a farmer professional gardener or a restorer of old houses, though also not a singer and, most definitely, not a voice teacher. Aptitude is only one qualifier. I am too damned malcontented and- even with a permanently sore testicle- too great a fussbudget for the former vocations, too easily knocked down for the latter. I am a quitter, someone who seldom sees things to the other side. Still, though possessing certain gray matter, I could never have concentrated on a more academic line. I am ADD or slightly Dyslexic, or a light Bi-Polar bear. Alas, my eventual high school mentor was only half right—or right about only half of *me*, or of *one* me. Only…. only I don't know what the other is, don't know who I am instead, who or what is my better half. Prithee, grant me a final appreciation for the wisdom of that truth. Or clearer lunacy.

Perhaps because we three didn't take enough time deciding on a life's course, me, myself, and I, are interested in precisely nothing we once were. We can't imagine what makes people want to sing for a living. We grew weary of our farm and were glad to unload it, were too stiff to work at something menial, hated the heat, felt no eventual abiding love for the cold. Call it normal aging, but….

I believe I did after all proceed from a nomadic tribe. In Germany, they would call me "*Zwischen Fach*," always in between, moving around. If in Kentucky, I'm ready for the city; if delighting over a board of sushi in New York, I long for biscuits and gravy in the country. My grade school love nailed it early on: fickle. I enjoy opera if done well, which it never is, but feel gagged with a spoon around singers. In my pants live ants, and not the kind you get rid of eating in the Asian restaurants I patronize.

Contemplating my literary self-destruction—ending my one and only book in such a goofy-assed way—is revolting. I like wine and a sip of "hooch". Sometimes I would "get off" on shuttling (the operative word) about the globe and like reviewing what I put in print; it helps my self-image. But….

I am actually going backward! I need a leave of absence, a break, from what, or to *do* what, I have no idea; I nonetheless need it. I told myself I don't mind the smell of cow shit. As the brilliant wacko in my New York apartment building would say, "THIS GODDAMMED COWSHIT! IT'S HARRIBLE!" *I am not the same.* I am ashamed of *I*; the finch-less suicide window is Calling! I…just…I tell you…. …. I …….. Say….

Say. Say, never mind where I was going with all that.

Say!

Say, I said something there. You know….. "you *know*," I said. You *do* know. I wonder… I wonder if there could be the slightest chance…. if I could ever be….. be a …\a…/….. *writer!* No, come on, I mean a **real** writer. Surely not. I'd have to grow up. Besides, I'd have discovered the capacity long ago, or someone else would've.

But. But what about it? What do *YOU* think? How long do I have? How long do *you* have? You could help me. Please! Help me. I need you. Do. **   //   ~~   ..>>==——   ++

Nah. What a crock. Forget I even mentioned it.

My neck and other arthritis hurt too much to sit at a damned computer all day the way some people do. Michener said that even late in life he couldn't wait to go to bed so he could get up and start writing again. I don't know how he did it. I'd spill coffee all over it anyway. I hurt enough sitting for two or three voice lessons, only then, of course, my ears pound as well. Besides what I said before, writers have to know so much, be so well read. You know? Sure, they sometimes do research, go for interviews with people then write based on that. But you have to like people. Figures: my favorite play was *The Misanthrope.*

I'm too behind still, see? Spent too long since grade school goofing off instead of building my knowledge, that and in a vocal practice room beating my head against the wall. Or sounding like it. Warming up in my hotel for a performance with the Atlanta Symphony once, the maid knocked on my door wanting to know if I was sick. See what I mean? I'm a misfit. I think I'm on the road to doing the same with my painting. Did I say I paint pictures?

I'd probably just....... It was a good thought, but...well... anyway...

Thanks for reading my book to the end. It means a lot to me. I hope you've enjoyed the accounting. Nothing if not in and out, like that Kentucky river fog, eh? If you did like it, though, tell your friends, even if you'll have no idea what to tell them. I know: tell them I tried to be truthful and not "lay" (ha") to them, though I did! You know it really is a kick, seeing what you wrote in print. A "gas," as we used to say in the 1960s. I am old fart.

Have a good life.* I have to go take my Lexapro now.

---

*Gary Kendall, ex-farmhand, ex-paper boy, ex-TV repairman, ex-water department laborer, ex-grocery stocker, ex-library science assistant, ex-rehabber of two houses, ex-gardener, ex-singer, ex-college professor, soon-to-be an ex-painter. Just call me a sometime private voice teacher who once wrote a bunch of pieces and bound them together.......Hasta la vista. Did I say I've been teaching myself Spanish?

Chapter Outline

<u>Introduction</u>: <u>Nature and True Nature</u>: An overview of my life, necessary for the understanding of the book as a whole beginning with small town/country living, up through life in New York, singing professionally, and teaching voice, both collegiate and private: "A second Call soon followed. It found me off fishing somewhere........ Ah, but switchboard operators didn't throw in the towel easily....."

<u>Prologue</u>: <u>Inhospitable Psychobabble</u>: A tongue-in-cheek genesis of the chapters in book form, blaming my wife, Arlene, for the whole project, namely by tricking me while under surgical anesthesia. Written in one the book's 'spoof' voices. In the process, gives more background and insight into me, the way my brain works, and what is coming, increasingly, throughout the book.........

<u>Sky King</u>: Profile of my jack-of-all-trades-though-master-of-several high school music teacher. Offers incidental insights into what a small town Missouri upbringing would and would not include, especially prejudices. Includes a posthumous apology for having neglected the person in question after I left home, though, oddly enough, we attended the same university together. He became Missouri Assistant Commissioner of Education.

<u>Around the Block in Eighty Days</u>: Moralistic close-up narrative of my childhood, ending with events from the early professional singing years, along with illustrations of why I was always playing catch up, namely that my family was too poor to travel: "Around the world in another eighty days, or years, and I might act like I had been there before... I had made a ton of mistakes.... leaving my parents to wonder if their baby had...been brought home by some wayward stork with the bird flu." The chapter could be considered another overview, though in more detail, for the early periods.

<u>With Tibor Once More:</u> Portrait of my most influential college professor, hated to this day at the school where he taught before his tragic and premature end; this essay is a paean to the man. It narrates his often-tragic life: from the murder of his fiancé by the Nazis, his talent, principles, discipline, and shortcomings, to the many things he taught me. Amounts to a cathartic exercise for me, since I went from being his favorite student singer, to someone about whom he wrote a scathing college placement file reference.

<u>Valhall-arious to Missile-aneous:</u> Long and true-story chapter, treating onstage (opera and concert) mishaps; also my own my willingness to do almost anything for a joke, with emphasis on why such things are funnier still when in live performance, or any other time one mustn't laugh. Drawn mostly from my student and early performing years. One incident—involving my giving a bogus translation of the Requiem Mass line, "Tuba Mirum, Spargens Sonum," just before my colleagues and I stood up to sing a rehearsal in Mexico—spawned the title of this book.

<u>Managing to Please:</u> Personal profile of the late great singers' agent, Joseph Lippman, with critical undercurrent of today's agent scene. Joe was most definitely one of a kind, also the last of *his* (professional and personal) kind. Chapter details why he wanted to be thought of as a manager, not an agent, what the difference is, and of the son he never had. I sat by his bedside until the day before he died. Said Joe to his doctor, "You can't let me die; my kids need me." We did, and the world, most definitely the singing world, has never been the same since.

<u>On My Watch:</u> Account of the wild and wonderful September of 1974. A philandering husband, I won The Geneva International Music Competition in singing. The chapter includes portraits and descriptions of interesting people and experiences *en route* to the competition's final round, their effect on me then, and how they tied in- or failed to- with aspects of my future.

<u>A Swallowty of Life Thing:</u> Personal profile of an "Haute Culture," and older, Swedish friend from the mid-1970s who influenced me greatly, and left me with many stories–his and my own. Chapter contains cogent commentary on parallel aspects of life in the 20th *and* 21st Century, of which my friend most definitely would not have approved: "A young woman sat behind the wheel of a minivan... stuffing the better part of a stuffed bagel into her mouth." Chapter has a "kicker" at the end.

<u>Thimik, Not Mimic:</u> Illustrated and partly comical piece about foreign language learning, and how my own tendency to mimic sounds without thinking would get me into social trouble: "Daddy, do your Chinese imitation for..." those two Chinese students that entered our train car. It ends with a naturally funny personal incident from my teaching years in Cincinnati, during which time I also purchased the farm in Kentucky. It applies an apt comparison to the Suzuki method of classical string instrument learning.

<u>Linville on Loan:</u> Through a biographical sketch of a wonderful Kentucky neighbor, this chapter paints life in "Farm Country, USA"; provides insights into people from that part of the world, what meeting them in a vehicle on your country road said about them, what I learned from them in general, and how important good neighbors are, especially to a novice farmer: "'He was a real guy' is the way I learned to say it in Kentucky Speak."

<u>Institutions of Lower Learning:</u> What music schools are really like, as told by a seeing and thinking person who has "been there." Amounts to a rather un-pretty picture of academia in general, in particular classical singing (voice) curricula, colleagues, "Generation X" and "Millennial" students, and what voice graduates leave any music school in this country not knowing. It is frank and a little inflammatory.

<u>Refrains from a K-9 *Chor*:</u> Country flavored accounting of my history with dogs, as paraphrased ("half read, half improvised") by a would-be local judge, nicknamed after a Kentucky Bourbon... "who I got married by when my leg was broke." Brings out more flavor of living on the Kentucky countryside, and specifics about the life and death of KoKo, a

black and tan German Shepherd who had sixteen pups in one litter; also what being awakened by their howling in the middle of the night was like. *"Chor"* translates to "chorus" in German.

Bearing Interest on a Practical Family Savings Plan: Sectional essay on historic preservation with a different slant, highlighting examples found in the country, where there are no preservation societies: "Mortals are…ships moving through deep waters. They… make their way against storm, and in calm waters... borrow a few things that they can't … take with them… pass them on, where or to whom no one is at all sure." Motivated by a *nouveau riche* family on my road that tore down a wonderful old brick home just because they didn't want to look at it.

Myself is Ashamed of We: the Amateurnouns of the Pros: Essay on basic grammatical mistakes of (professional) talking heads: " 'My wife and myself are having twins.' Yikes! Myself is exponentially reproducing." Contains several examples of people who simply should know better, including those uttered in faculty meetings at University of Cincinnati. Refers to my penchant for English grammar, passed on by my mother, and how easy that part of high school was for me, since I never studied; also my teacher's annoyance with me for it.

Clear Sailing and Omelet-Present Danger: Comical depiction of the dangers in being a creature of habit, especially one walking the streets of New York City on the way to breakfast; initiates book-long theme of medical-world and New York life satire, poking fun at the typical super "into their stuff" New Age New Yorkers, no different from what they were before their conversions, despite the great new methods they now swear by. Contains detailed close-up story of the extremely painful but funny fix I got into, especially on a cruise ship, while suffering from testicular area inflammation.

November *Attacca*: The Italian word for both "attach" and "attack," it is used in classical music to indicate continuing without pause between sections or movements of compositions. In this case, it is a *double entendre*, signifying a short sequel to the previous chapter: "Our time-worn restaurant has lost its lease," and the sentimental but slightly dangerous event I encounter chancing by the old haunt, yet demonstrating that I was "home again," and that all was well.

Taking One to Know One to No One: A more-than-one-man sad saga about someone I should have been much closer to, but neglected for most of his entire long life; continues underlying self-deprecating theme, serious or tongue-in-cheek; also of societal decadence. The surprise of the first page is what my relationship to the man was. His body was discovered in the bedroom of a tiny mobile home, with no air conditioning, during a record Arizona heat wave. It describes how his passing affected, and failed to affect, me: "He died last month. The name was Lynch, age 89. It was in a small town, not far from the California state line. But I *don't* know who."

The Vast Left Lane Conspiracy: One page lecture from one who drives fifty thousand miles per year, in specific, battling drivers who get out in the left lane and "park" while still moving. With comical undertone, and story from a friend who teaches English As A Second Language to adults, as well as a childhood memory of a friend pulled over for running a stop sign. The chapter should "feel" familiar to anyone who dares get on Interstate Highways.

Teaching From the Inside Out: A second person, mostly true story about the perils of classical voice teaching (or coaching) at home, even in New York–the city that never sleeps–where traditionally anything goes during normal hours. It provides close-ups of sorts on New York apartment dwelling in general, and of obsessing on one particular neighbor; bittersweet, if funny.

Again, The Voice: A free-style poem I wrote, and read on the occasion of the memorial service for a particularly great student of mine who died after a severe bi-polar episode.

A Finch in Time Saves Mine: Flashback story within a story of my years on the Kentucky farm and what became my "critter connection," wild and domesticated; ends with a corny but touching freeform poem to the house finch that inspired the story, sitting on the air conditioner looking (*Nevermore*) into my New York "*chamber*." Makes a convincing case for country living: what it centers on, the excitement always brewing, and where something is always going awry. The chapter should be poignant to any animal lover.

<u>Refluxions From A Gut Level</u>: Part tongue-in-cheek/satirical and historical accounting of ailments, especially of the typical hypochondriacal classical singer. It details the latest medical rage at the time of writing, gastrointestinal reflux. Though slanted toward opera singers, it imparts good advice for anyone else. Gives insight into singers' lives and personalities, and why their health is so important. It provides detailed information about reflux, the condition many people still don't know much about, and how problematic especially it is for singers.

<u>Taking Leave for My Senses</u>: Mostly spoof piece about the way we change, personally and medically; includes case study relating to my first academic leave of absence (sabbatical), and ends with a joke about going to "hell."

<u>For Sale by Owner</u>: Following a brief explanation, this chapter is a replica of a magazine/online ad for my farm property, once I decided to sell. The ad sold the property, giving a good description of what I did to improve it through the years, of the particular Kentucky area in general, and what it looks like, inside and out. Bittersweet.

<u>Showing Up a Minstrel Show</u>: Account of my life-long love/hate for classical singing/singers, of being one, my career woes moreover, and the neuroses it tended to trigger; ends with narrative of my family-motivated coming out of retirement for a performance, and of the involuntary patterns awakened thereby, after not performing for almost a decade and having nothing to lose. Ending is mock-serious.

<u>Twenty to Life in a Phone Cell</u>: Whacko sketch, re: living in the age of the ubiquitous cell phone, and what it says about us: " **'MOM? WE'RE AT GRISTEDES! THE GROCERY STORE...... NO, MY CELL ...YOU SURE?...OKAY.'** " She turns

around, apologizes for bashing me with her cart before the phone rings, but says nothing about sending me to my ENT for eardrum replacement." Chapter signals the beginning of a fictitious and emotional unraveling, though containing all true incidents involving cell phone use, blended with semi-fictional dream.

That Rotten Something in the State of Opera: Pretty much self-explanatory essay of one man's analysis pertaining to the production of opera as we approach it today, and from one who has enough experience to make a valid case. Details what is wrong: from what the approach emphasizes and doesn't, how badly even that part is done, why it bankrupts the organizations, and why we therefore don't have the great singing of past ages.
Poem.

Retort To Retort: A response to the D.H. Lawrence poem, "Retort to Jesus." Is an iconoclastic comment on what I feel is our all too prevalent in our politically correct society.

Beneath the Doric Columnist: "Inspiration-less" summary of who I am, and what is beneath my many layers. Contains spoof genesis for the (fictional) next chapter (Old Popes Never Die), and my non-life as a newspaper columnist. Draws analogy to President Nixon's famous eighteen-minute tape gap, and to my newspaper column when the newspaper—run by a drunk—folded. Written in a stream-of-consciousness, parodying manner, that ends with a plain, numbered list of things that piss me off. Contains the strongest signal yet of my essay-and-vignette form of progressive hysteria.

Old Popes Never Die, Just Fade from Pew: (Or: The Instant-Bull, Constantin-Popal Conflap). Make-believe and totally fictional one act play of pope standing before God: "Put your hand down and stop stirring up the air. I designed that sign for the Native American long before you were born." Is a humorous but inflammatory essay for any Catholic without a sense of humor. Contains at least one flashback character (my mother) from an earlier chapter, and satire of certain beliefs and political events: "But keep to the right. The room on the left is the 'Ecstasy Room' reserved for Bill and Monica."

Artists' Digest and the Classic American Popsicle: Critical treatise on the curious contradiction in taste amongst people in visual arts and other branches of organized erudition when it comes to music. Ends with an example of a prominent, learned man, who happens to be the real life villain in the chapter, "Teaching from the Inside Out." Chapter contains what I believe to be rarely considered artistic food for thought.

Wrens On My Yard Art: Semi-spoof reflecting philosophical thoughts of art, what constitutes it, and the role buying and selling may play. In keeping with (imaginary) frustrations of a ne'er-do-well, the increasing literary style of tying in recurring themes from previous vignettes, and a tongue-in-cheek increasing apparent hysteria and reason for the book. Triggered again by a bird, seeing a pair of Carolina wrens on the yard sculpture I fashioned from objects left in our yard by the previous owner.

Mastering "Lie," "Lay," and "Lain": Using more character flashback and literary *"Leitmotif"* from other chapters, sums up what eventually "became" this book, though in a surprising way; is a "sketch" in more than one sense, progressing increasingly - if tongue-in-cheek faux hysteria the end. Culminates with the groundswell of a big admission, ideas for what I might do when I "grow up," taking depression medicine, thanking my readers, and signing off with a list of the former jobs and titles of a lifelong misfit (me).

Author

As his publisher description indicates, Gary Kendall was a born-and-bred cranky kid from a religious mid-western family. Due to the time period and location, he is safe roaming about on his own, so that the lion's share of his boyhood lessons stem from the *Wanderlust* itself.

He excels in music but doesn't see much of an emphasis around him for academics, and flounders, yet chooses college at graduation time. From hunting and farm work, he strays into areas not really right for him, then devotes later years to circling back—literally and figuratively—from halfway around the world.

Long time friends muse on the raging young man he once was, while his Face Book profile eventually points up such interests as linguistics, painting, handyman work, cooking, writer, singing, teaching, horsemanship, studious sidelines, and wise-cracking.

The work herein spot-checks all the above and more, in a style predictably crossed amongst classical music performance, a return to the land, pet peeves, self-honesty struggles, regrets, and a host of other elements that he, least of all, would have expected in any seventy-five-year span.

Made in the USA
Columbia, SC
27 May 2020